License to Cook Minnesota Style

by Gerry Kangas

About the Author: Gerry Kangas of Aurora, Minnesota has been involved with food as long as she can remember. Her mother cooked at logging camps in Northern Minnesota and Gerry spent several summers with her in the kitchen. Gerry and her husband owned and managed a board and lodging home for over twenty years. Their reputation was built on "Good Home Cooking." Gerry has coordinated ethnic food demonstrations, including the American Folk Life Festival in Washington, D.C., sponsored by the Smithsonian Institution.

Edited by Michelle Nagle Spencer, Helga Matt Stevens, Juanita J. Loven, Georgia Heald, Hannelore Liffring-Zug Bourret.

Front cover designed by Dana Lumby. Drawings

ISBN 1-57216-028-4   Copyright © 2004 Penfield Books

Contents

Marvelous Minnesota	4
Wild Rice	7
Blueberries and Other Wild Fruits	30
Apples	44
Beverages and Snacks	54
Soups, Stews, Sauces, and Salads	60
Breads	74
Fish, Meat, Poultry, and Wild Game	84
Vegetables and Side Dishes	119
Desserts and Cookies	129
A State of Events and Places to Visit	144
St. Urho's Day	158
Paul Bunyan	159

Marvelous Minnesota

By Dianne Stevens

Whether you are looking for culture or fishing, bright lights or boundary waters canoeing, wildlife or night life, warm summers or cold winters, Minnesota has it all.

Right in the heart of North America is a place many folks swear is heaven on earth. The first white explorers heard the Dakota Sioux Indians refer to this land as "Minisota"–the land of sky-tinted waters.

Minnesota today lives up to that label with much of its boundaries being water. The northern border includes Lake of the Woods, Rainy River, Rainy Lake, Namakan Lake, Loon Lake, Lac la Croix, Saganaga Lake, Boundary Canoe Waters, and Pigeon River. The eastern border includes Lake Superior and the St. Louis, St. Croix, and Mississippi Rivers. The western border includes the Red River of the North, the Bois de Sioux River, the Mud, Traverse, and Big Stone lakes and the Minnesota River. Iowa is the southern border.

(continued)

Marvelous Minnesota *(continued)*

If you are in Minnesota, you are close to water. There are 12,034 lakes of at least 10 acres. In northeast Minnesota the famous Boundary Waters Canoe Area Wilderness stretches for 150 magnificent miles. The Mississippi River starts in Itasca State Park (north of Park Rapids and southwest of Bemidji) and flows north before turning south, while the Minnesota River makes a bee-line southeast almost to Iowa before changing its mind and flowing northeast to join the Mississippi at St. Paul. Duluth is the largest inland port in the world. Lakes lure countless vacationers, and even with all that water there is plenty of room for the four million people who call Minnesota home. Half of those Minnesotans are living in the Twin Cities area—in and around St. Paul and Minneapolis. Native Americans, first the Laurel, then the Dakota (Sioux) and Ojibwa (Chippewa), were the first Minnesotans. State bird: Loon. Nicknames: North Star State, Gopher State. State flower: Lady's-slipper. State tree: Norway red pine.

(continued)

Marvelous Minnesota *(continued)*

One-fourth of all Minnesotans have Scandinavian roots, although German-Americans outnumber any other single ethnic group. Finns, Poles, French, Canadians, Dutch, Flemish, Icelanders, Danes, Jews, Swiss, Irish, Scots, Italians, Czechoslovakians, Asians, Hispanics, and others chose Minnesota, joining Native Americans to lend their heritage to the state's cultural diversity. At the Minnesota city market the Hmong sell vegetables and their renowned folk art embroidery from the same table. From the grand St. Paul Festival of Nations representing 73 ethnic groups, to the many Oktoberfests and smaller ethnic celebrations like Kolacky Days (named for a Czech delicacy) in Montgomery, the fingerprints of Minnesota's heritage are clear.

Festivals and wilderness areas are a large part of life in Minnesota, and don't forget the museums, theaters, and art galleries for culture, amusement parks for fun, and historical sites for a glimpse into Minnesota's past.

Whatever your tastes, dish up some Minnesota and enjoy.

Wild Rice

Baked Wild Rice	9	Spinach-Wild Rice Quiche	17
Baked Ham, Wild Rice, and Mushrooms	19	Steeped Wild Rice	10
		Summer Salad	11
Chicken Breast Stuffed with Wild Rice	24	The Wild Rice of Minnesota	8
		Wild Rice and Broccoli	18
Chicken Wild Rice Pilaf	23	Wild Rice Au Gratin	21
Cooked Wild Rice	9	Wild Rice-Beef Casserole	25
Creamy Wild Rice Soup	14	Wild Rice Bread	15
Ira's Wild Rice Casserole	22	Wild Rice Dressing	29
Microwaved Wild Rice	10	Wild Rice Party Salad	12
Popped Parched Wild Rice	13	Wild Rice Turkey Soufflé	27

The Wild Rice of Minnesota

It was known to the ancients, the Native Americans, the voyageurs, and now us. It is wild rice, the bounteous cereal grain of the northern waters, as nutritious as it is tasty. Minnesota is the home of wild rice, producing nearly five million pounds a year. The name "wild rice" is correct, but this rice can be tamed. Much of it is now grown in paddies and harvested with big machines.

Wild rice is related to the grasses, not to white or brown rice. But its special flavor caused the early explorers to call it a rice. It's excellent in or with meat, casseroles, soups, salads, breads, and vegetables. It's high in protein and fiber, low in fat and calories: 103 calories in a cup of cooked wild rice.

The wonders of wild rice became known throughout the nation as a result of its use by gourmet cooks.

Cooked Wild Rice

1 cup wild rice
3 cups cold water or broth
1 teaspoon salt
butter

Rinse rice thoroughly and cover with cold water. Add salt; cook 25 to 30 minutes until tender and most of liquid is absorbed. Serve with butter. Makes 3 cups.

Baked Wild Rice

1 cup wild rice
3 cups hot water
3 teaspoons chicken or beef bouillon granules

Rinse rice thoroughly and place in a casserole. Combine water and bouillon; pour over rice. Bake, covered, at 350° for 1 hour. Makes 3 cups.

Microwaved Wild Rice

1 cup wild rice
3 cups hot water
3 teaspoons chicken or beef bouillon granules

Rinse rice thoroughly and place in a microwavable dish. Combine water and bouillon; pour over rice. Cook, covered, on high for 15 to 30 minutes turning every 5 minutes to cook evenly, until most of the liquid is absorbed and rice is tender. Makes 3 cups.

Steeped Wild Rice

1 cup wild rice
boiling water
1 tablespoon salt
1 to 2 teaspoons butter, optional

Rinse rice thoroughly. Pour 3 cups boiling water over rice and let stand for 30 minutes; drain. Repeat 3 more times. Stir in salt and place rice in the top of a double boiler to keep hot. Serve with butter if desired. Makes 3 cups.

Summer Salad

1 cup wild rice
1 1/2 cups mayonnaise
1/4 cup plain yogurt
1/2 cup sliced celery

1 cup cubed tomatoes
1/2 cup diced cucumber
1 tablespoon chopped parsley
salt and pepper
shredded cheese or nuts

Cook rice. Mix with next six ingredients; season to taste. Cover and chill. Serve garnished with cheese or nuts. Serves 6.

Wild Rice Party Salad
Vera Johnson, Silver Bay, Minnesota

1 cup wild rice, cooked
1 12-ounce package macaroni rings, cooked
2 4 1/2 ounce cans shrimp bits and pieces
1 to 2 cups cubed ham
1 cup chopped onions
1/2 cup stuffed olives, sliced
1 cup chopped celery
1 to 2 cups shredded Cheddar cheese
1 cup chopped green pepper
4 ounces slivered almonds

Dressing:
1 cup salad dressing
1/2 cup sour cream
2 teaspoons sugar
milk
2 teaspoons vinegar

Place rice and macaroni in a large bowl. Add remaining ingredients and toss.
Dressing: Blend ingredients together, using milk to thin to desired consistency. Pour over salad and chill. Serves 10.

Popped Parched Wild Rice

Ira White, Mt. Iron, Minnesota

An Ojibwa Indian, the late Mr. White, with his family parched and sold wild rice. He was a former Indian agent of the Bois Forte, Nett Lake. It is essential to use only hand-parched rice for popping; commercially processed wild rice will not pop.

hand-parched wild rice	oil
	salt

Place a small amount of unwashed rice in a small wire strainer. Heat oil to 365°. Dip the strainer holding the parched rice into hot oil to pop. Drain popped rice on brown paper. Salt to taste. Serve popped rice with chow mein, as cereal, or as snack food.

Creamy Wild Rice Soup

Carol Tynjala, Aurora, Minnesota

2 tablespoons butter
1 tablespoon minced onion
1/4 cup flour
4 cups chicken broth

2 cups cooked wild rice
1/2 teaspoon salt
1 cup half-and-half
2 tablespoons dry sherry
chives or parsley, chopped

Sauté onion in butter until tender. Blend in flour. Gradually add broth, stirring constantly. Cook until mixture thickens slightly; add salt and rice. Simmer 5 minutes. Blend in half-and-half and sherry. Heat to serving temperature. Garnish with chives or parsley. Serves 4.

Wild Rice Bread

1/3 cup wild rice
1 package dry yeast
lukewarm water
1/4 cup brown sugar
1/4 cup molasses
1 tablespoon salt
1/4 cup oil or butter, softened
1/4 cup instant potato flakes
7 to 8 cups flour, divided
melted butter for tops

Thoroughly rinse rice. Cover with water and boil until tender, about 25 minutes. Drain and reserve liquid. Dissolve yeast in 1/4 cup lukewarm water. Add enough lukewarm water to reserved liquid to make 2 1/4 cups. Combine liquid, yeast mixture, brown sugar, molasses, salt, oil, potato flakes, and 2 cups flour in a large bowl. Beat until smooth. Add drained wild rice and enough additional flour to make a soft dough. Place

(continued)

Wild Rice Bread *(continued)*

on a floured board and knead for 5 to 10 minutes. Place in a greased bowl, cover, and let rise for 2 hours or until double in bulk. Punch down and let rise again. Shape into 3 loaves and place in 3 well-greased, 9x5-inch loaf pans. Let rise until sides reach top of pan and center is well rounded, about 50 to 60 minutes. Bake at 375° for 45 to 50 minutes. Remove from pans and brush tops with butter.

Spinach-Wild Rice Quiche

3 eggs, divided
1 1/2 cups hot, cooked wild rice
3 ounces cheese, grated, divided
3/4 teaspoon salt

2 1/4 cups thawed frozen spinach, well drained
3 tablespoons skim milk
1/8 teaspoon pepper
1 cup sliced mushrooms

Beat 1 egg; stir in rice, half the cheese, and salt. Press firmly into an even layer on the bottom of a 9-inch pie, cake or quiche pan. Beat remaining eggs; stir in spinach, milk, pepper, mushrooms, and remaining cheese. Spoon into pan. Bake at 375° for 30 minutes or until cooked through. Cool 15 minutes before serving. Serves 3.

Wild Rice and Broccoli

3/4 cup wild rice
1 cup sliced celery
2 10-ounce packages frozen broccoli spears, cooked
3 tablespoons butter

3 tablespoons flour
1/4 teaspoon salt
1 chicken bouillon cube, crushed
2 cups milk
1/2 cup Parmesan cheese, divided
1 tablespoon lemon juice

Cook rice; stir in celery. Spoon mixture into a greased, shallow, 2-quart casserole. Arrange broccoli over rice mixture. In a small saucepan, melt butter, add flour, salt, and bouillon. Gradually add milk, stirring constantly until mixture becomes thick and smooth. Stir in 1/4 cup cheese and lemon juice. Pour over broccoli. Sprinkle with remaining cheese. Bake at 375° for 20 minutes. Serves 6 to 8.

Baked Ham, Wild Rice, and Mushrooms

1 cup wild rice
2 1/2 cups water
1 1/2 cups diced ham
4 tablespoons bacon drippings, divided, optional
1/4 pound mushrooms, sliced
1 rib celery, diced
1 cup chopped onion
3 tablespoons flour
2 1/2 cups milk
salt and pepper to taste
1/2 cup fine dry bread crumbs
1 tablespoon melted butter

Rinse rice. Bring water to a boil in an uncovered saucepan. Cook rice in boiling water for about 25 minutes until firm tender and all the water is absorbed. Meanwhile brown ham in 2 tablespoons of bacon drippings. Add mushrooms, celery, and onion; cook about 10 minutes. Spoon into a 1 1/2-quart casserole. In a small saucepan, blend flour

(continued)

Baked Ham, Wild Rice, and Mushrooms *(continued)*

with the remaining bacon drippings, heat until bubbly. Add milk, salt, and pepper; cook, stirring constantly until thick and smooth. Pour over ham mixture. Add rice and toss lightly to mix. Combine crumbs and melted butter. Sprinkle over casserole. Bake, uncovered, at 350° for about 45 minutes or until rice is tender and top is browned. Serves 4 to 6.

Wild Rice Au Gratin

1 cup wild rice
2 cups sliced fresh mushrooms

3 tablespoons butter
2 cups grated Cheddar cheese

Cook rice. Sauté mushrooms in butter until tender. Combine rice, mushrooms, and cheese; pour into a 2-quart casserole. Bake, covered, at 325° for 20 minutes. Uncover and bake an additional 10 minutes. Serves 8 as a side dish.

Ira's Wild Rice Casserole
Mrs. Ira White, Mt. Iron, Minnesota

1 1/2 cups wild rice
cold water
1/2 pound pork, cubed
1/2 pound beef, cubed
1 tablespoon oil

1 cup water
salt to taste
1 14 1/2-ounce can tomatoes
1 4-ounce can mushrooms
1 small onion, diced

Wash and drain rice. Cover with cold water and cook for 25 minutes. Brown the meats in oil. Add remaining ingredients except rice and simmer for 20 minutes. Stir in rice and pour into a covered casserole. Bake, covered, for 1 hour at 325°. Serves 4.

Chicken Wild Rice Pilaf

1 medium-sized onion, diced
1/2 cup chopped celery
2 tablespoons butter or margarine

1/4 cup chopped sweet red pepper
2 cups cooked wild rice
2 cups cooked diced chicken
salt and pepper to taste

Sauté onion and celery in butter until tender. Stir in remaining ingredients. Season to taste. Heat through. Serves 4.

Chicken Breast Stuffed with Wild Rice

1/2 cup wild rice
1 1/2 cups chicken broth
2 medium-sized onions, chopped
1 4-ounce can mushrooms

2 tablespoons butter or margarine
salt and pepper to taste
4 chicken breasts
soy sauce, for basting
melted butter, for basting

Cook wild rice in chicken broth. Sauté onions and mushrooms in butter until tender. Add wild rice and season to taste. Bone chicken breasts and pound each one flat. Place rice mixture on each breast; roll and fasten with skewers. Baste with soy sauce and melted butter. Broil until brown on both sides. Bake, covered, at 350° for 45 minutes or until tender. Serves 4.

Wild Rice-Beef Casserole

1 cup wild rice
4 cups water
1 tablespoon salt
1 pound ground beef
1/2 cup chopped onion

1/4 cup minced green pepper
1 cup chopped celery
1/2 cup water
1 1-quart can tomatoes
salt and pepper to taste

Wash wild rice thoroughly and place in a heavy saucepan with 4 cups water and salt. Bring to a boil; reduce heat and simmer, covered, for 45 minutes, until tender, but not mushy. Uncover and fluff with a fork. Simmer for an additional 5 minutes. Brown beef. Add onion and green pepper; cook until vegetables are tender. Cook celery in 1/2 cup water. In a casserole, combine rice, celery, tomatoes, meat mixture, and seasonings. Bake at 350° for 30 minutes. Serves 8 to 10.

Wild Rice Meatballs
Turna Saarberg, Aurora, Minnesota

1 pound ground beef
1 small onion, finely chopped
1/2 cup cooked wild rice
1/2 teaspoon seasoned salt
1/2 teaspoon garlic salt
1/3 cup fine dry bread crumbs
1/2 cup evaporated milk

1 10 3/4-ounce can cream of mushroom soup
1/2 soup can of water
1/2 soup can of dry white wine
1/2 teaspoon salt
1/4 teaspoon sage
black pepper to taste

Combine beef, onion, rice, seasoned and garlic salts, bread crumbs, and milk. Shape into 1-inch balls; place in a jellyroll pan. Bake at 375° for 10 to 15 minutes, or until browned. Combine soup, water, wine, and spices in a saucepan; heat. Add meatballs and simmer for 1/2 hour. Serves 4.

Wild Rice Turkey Soufflé
Minnesota Turkey Growers Association

3 cups cooked wild rice
4 cups cooked diced turkey
1/2 cup chopped celery
1/2 cup chopped onion

Mushroom Sauce:
2 large eggs, beaten
1 1/2 cups milk

Topping:

1/2 cup chopped green pepper
1/2 cup mayonnaise
1 4-ounce can mushroom pieces
3/4 teaspoon salt
dash pepper

1 10 3/4-ounce can cream of
　　mushroom soup, undiluted

1/3 cup shredded Cheddar cheese

(continued)

Wild Rice Turkey Soufflé

(continued)

Line a greased 9x13-inch baking dish with rice. Combine remaining ingredients. Spread evenly over rice.
Mushroom Sauce: Blend all ingredients until smooth. Pour over turkey mixture.
Topping: Sprinkle with cheese. Refrigerate for 1 hour. Bake at 350° for 1 hour. Serves 10.

Wild rice

Wild Rice Dressing

1 cup wild rice
giblets, cooked and chopped
2 cups broth
1/2 cup finely chopped onion

2 1/2 cups finely chopped celery
1/2 cup butter or margarine
8 cups seasoned bread cubes
2 eggs, lightly beaten

Rinse wild rice; cover with water and boil about 25 minutes until firm tender. Combine rice, giblets, and broth. Sauté onions and celery in butter until lightly browned. Mix all ingredients thoroughly. Use within 24 hours. Makes 15 cups.
Variations: Add sherry or white wine to taste. Add 1 cup slivered almonds, toasted in butter, 1 cup browned mushrooms, or bits of crisp bacon.

Blueberries and Other Wild Fruits

Blueberry Bars	40
Blueberry Nut Bread	38
Chokecherry	33
Extracting Fruit Juice	31
Five-Minute Fresh Wild Blueberry Pie	43
Gooseberry Jelly	34
Highbush Cranberry Jello	36
Lo-Cal Blueberry Syrup	39
North Woods Blueberry Pancakes	42
Wild Pincherry	35
Wild Plum Jam	37

Norway Red Pine
Minnesota state tree

Extracting Fruit Juice

Minnesota Extension Service, University of Minnesota

Extraction of fruit juice from the fruit is the first step in the preparation of fruit syrup and fruit jelly. If extracting juice for use in syrup of pectin-added jelly, use ripe fruit or berries. If the juice is to be used for traditional long-boil method jelly, use 1/4 under-ripe and 3/4 ripe fruit. Wash fruit. Crush berries and cut up larger fruit before cooking. See the table on the next page for suggested amounts of water and cooking times per pound. Most fruit gives 1 to 1 1/3 cups juice per pound of fruit. Highbush cranberries, crabapples, chokecherries, and rose hips give close to 2 cups per pound of fruit. **Warning: Remove seeds of chokecherries and pincherries.**

(continued)

(continued)

Fruit	Water per pound of fruit	Cooking time* (Covered pot)
Blackberries	1/4 cup	5 to 10 minutes
Chokecherries **remove seeds**	water to cover	15 minutes or until soft
Crabapples	water to cover	20 to 25 minutes
Currants	1/2 cup	10 to 15 minutes
Gooseberries	1/4 cup	5 to 10 minutes
Highbush cranberries	3 cups	3 to 5 minutes
Pincherries **remove seeds**	1/2 cup	5 to 10 minutes
Rose hips	water to cover	15 minutes or until soft
Wild grapes	1 cup	5 to 10 minutes

*Bring to a boil, then simmer.

DO NOT crush the seed of chokecherries or pincherries. These seeds contain cyanide-forming compounds which can cause illness or death if eaten in large amounts. Pincherries and chokecherries are Minnesota favorites and **seeds must be removed.**

Chokecherry

Minnesota Extension Service, University of Minnesota

Syrup

4 cups chokecherry juice
seeds removed

4 cups sugar
1/2 cup lemon juice
1/2 package powdered pectin

Mix and boil ingredients for 2 minutes. Process jars of syrup 10 minutes in boiling water bath, as per manufacturer's directions.

Jelly

3 cups chokecherry juice
seeds removed

6 1/2 cups sugar
1 bottle liquid pectin
1/4 teaspoon almond extract

Pour juice into a large heavy kettle. Add sugar and stir to mix. Bring to a boil, stirring constantly. Stir in pectin. Bring to a full rolling boil and boil hard 1 minute, stirring constantly. Remove from heat. Stir and skim 3 minutes. Add almond extract. Pour into hot sterilized jars. Seal.

Gooseberry Jelly

2 1/2 cups juice from green gooseberries

2 1/2 cups juice from ripe gooseberries

5 cups sugar

Combine juice and sugar. Bring to a boil and boil until the temperature reaches 220° to 222° or until jelly sheets from spoon. Remove from heat and skim off foam. Pour into hot, sterilized jars and seal.

Wild Pincherry

Minnesota Extension Service, University of Minnesota

Syrup

2 cups wild pincherry juice, **seeds removed**
3 cups sugar
1/2 cup white corn syrup

Bring ingredients to a boil in a large saucepan. Turn down heat and simmer 15 minutes. Pour into hot sterilized jars. Seal jars in a water bath for 10 minutes or as per manufacturer's directions.

Jelly

6 1/2 cups pincherry juice, **seeds removed**
7 cups sugar
1 box powdered pectin

Combine all ingredients in a kettle and bring to a full rolling boil. Boil hard for 1 minute, stirring constantly. Remove from heat, skim off foam, pour into hot sterilized jars and seal.

Highbush Cranberry Jelly

2 cups highbush cranberry juice	1 1/2 cups sugar

Combine juice and sugar. Heat mixture until sugar dissolves. Boil over high heat until jelly sheets from spoon or until temperature reaches 220° to 222°. Remove from heat and skim off foam. Pour into hot sterilized containers and seal.

Highbush cranberry

Wild Plum Jam

Minnesota Extension Service, University of Minnesota

3 cups wild plums, pitted and mashed

6 cups sugar
1 box powdered pectin
1 cup water

Combine fruit and sugar. Let stand about 20 minutes, stirring occasionally. Boil powdered pectin and water rapidly for 1 minute, stirring constantly. Remove from heat. Add the fruit and stir about 2 minutes. Pour into jars; tighten lids. Let stand at room temperature for 24 hours or until jellied. Store in freezer or refrigerator. Makes 9 cups.

Blueberry Nut Bread

- 3 cups flour
- 1 teaspoon salt
- 4 teaspoons baking powder
- 2 eggs, beaten
- 1 cup sugar
- 1 cup milk
- 3 tablespoons melted shortening or oil
- 2 cups fresh blueberries
- walnuts to taste

Sift together flour, salt, and baking powder. Combine eggs and sugar; mix thoroughly. Blend milk and shortening with egg mixture. Add dry ingredients and stir only until blended. Fold in blueberries and walnuts carefully. Pour into a large greased loaf pan and bake at 350° for 1 hour.

Lo-Cal Blueberry Syrup

1 cup blueberries
1/2 cup unsweetened apple juice
1 cinnamon stick

1 teaspoon cornstarch
2 teaspoons water
1/2 teaspoon vanilla

Combine blueberries and juice in a blender and blend. Pour the mixture into a saucepan with cinnamon stick; bring to a boil over medium heat. Mix cornstarch and water; add to blueberry mixture. Boil for 2 minutes, stirring constantly. Add vanilla. Cool slightly and use as a topping for pancakes, French toast, or waffles.

Blueberry Bars

Dough:
1 cup butter or margarine, softened
1 cup granulated sugar

1 teaspoon vanilla
2 eggs
2 cups sifted flour

Filling:
2 cups fresh blueberries

1/2 cup sugar

Topping:
1 egg

1/4 cup sugar
1/2 cup coconut, chopped walnuts
   or pecans

(continued)

Blueberry Bars *(continued)*

Dough: Cream butter and sugar. Beat in vanilla and eggs. Mix in flour until a soft dough is formed. Press 1/2 the dough into a 9x13-inch baking dish, this layer will be very thin.
Filling: Cover layer of dough with berries and sprinkle with sugar. Cover berry layer with remaining dough, spreading dough evenly over berries.
Topping: Beat egg until foamy; add sugar. Spread over dough layer. Sprinkle with chopped nuts. Bake at 350° for 40 to 45 minutes. Cool and cut into bars.
Note: Raspberries or a combination of blueberries and raspberries can be used.

North Woods Blueberry Pancakes

2 eggs, beaten
1/2 cup sugar
1/4 cup shortening, melted
2 cups buttermilk
1 teaspoon baking soda
1/2 teaspoon salt
2 cups flour
1 to 2 cups blueberries

Beat together all ingredients except blueberries. Fry batter on a lightly greased griddle, adding 1 tablespoon of blueberries to the first side before turning. Brown on both sides and stack on a warm plate. Makes about 24 pancakes.

Five-Minute Fresh Wild Blueberry Pie

3 cups wild blueberries, divided
1 cup sugar
juice of one lemon

4 tablespoons water, divided
2 heaping tablespoons cornstarch
1 9-inch baked pie shell
whipped cream

Combine 1 cup blueberries, sugar, lemon juice, and 2 tablespoons water. Bring to a boil and cook for 3 minutes. Dissolve cornstarch in remaining water; add. Simmer until thickened. Remove from heat and stir in remaining blueberries. Pour into baked pie shell. Chill. Serve with whipped cream.

Apples

Apple Cake with Rum Sauce	49
Daffy Apple Salad	46
German Apple Torte	48
Kuchen	51
Sour Cream Apple Squares	47
The Apples of Minnesota	45
Yummy Apple Muffins	53

Split Rock Lighthouse,
Lake Superior

The Apples of Minnesota

Southeast Minnesota is the apple capital of the state. There are also orchards in the area of the Twin Cities, and elsewhere. The favorite apple is the Haralson, a tasty variety developed at the University of Minnesota for northern orchards. Many varieties are grown, including Delicious, McIntosh, Connell Red, and others. Most orchards have several varieties; at some you can pick your own right from the trees. Apple cider is for sale at most orchards, and at many orchards apple pie and other apple delicacies, such as doughnuts and muffins, are offered. For apple news call the Minnesota Travel Information Center at 1-888-TOURISM (868-7476) or, in the Twin Cities, 651-296-5029. See also: www.exploreminnesota.com. The free *Minnesota Grown Directory* lists locations of orchards, produce farms, and farmers' markets. Or write to the Minnesota Office of Tourism, 100 Metro Square, 121 Seventh Place E., St. Paul, Minnesota 55101.

Daffy Apple Salad
Julie Turk, Aurora, Minnesota

1 tablespoon flour
1/2 cup sugar
1 8-ounce can crushed pineapple, drained, juice reserved
1 egg
2 tablespoons apple cider vinegar
4 cups pared apple chunks, chilled
1 8-ounce package whipped topping
1 cup salted peanuts, divided

Combine flour, sugar, pineapple juice, egg, and vinegar in a saucepan and stir over medium heat until very thick. Refrigerate mixture until very cold. Add apples to cold sauce. Fold in pineapple, whipped topping, and 1/2 cup peanuts. Pour into a serving bowl and garnish with remaining peanuts. Serve cold.

Sour Cream Apple Squares

Luella Maki, Ely, Minnesota

Luella won the Pillsbury Bakeoff with this recipe.

- 2 cups flour
- 2 cups firmly packed brown sugar
- 1/2 cup butter or margarine, softened
- 1 cup chopped nuts
- 1 to 2 teaspoons cinnamon
- 1 teaspoon baking soda
- 1/2 teaspoon salt
- 1 cup sour cream
- 1 teaspoon vanilla
- 1 egg
- 2 cups peeled, finely chopped apples
- whipped cream

Combine flour, sugar, and butter; blend until crumbly. Stir in nuts. Press 2 3/4 cups of the flour mixture into an ungreased 9x13-inch baking dish. Add cinnamon, baking soda, salt, sour cream, vanilla, and egg to remaining mixture; blend well. Stir in apples. Spoon evenly over flour layer. Bake at 350° for 25 to 35 minutes, or until toothpick inserted in the center comes out clean. Cut into squares. Serve with whipped cream. Makes 12 to 15.

German Apple Torte
Ironworld USA, Chisholm, Minnesota

1/2 cup plus 2 tablespoons butter
  or margarine
3/4 cup sugar, divided
2 eggs
1 teaspoon grated lemon rind

1 1/2 cups flour
1 1/4 teaspoons baking powder
1 1/2 to 2 pounds tart apples,
  peeled, quartered and cut in
  ribs on the rounded edges
whipped cream

Cream butter and 1/2 cup sugar. Beat in eggs one at a time. Add lemon rind. Stir in flour and baking powder. Pour batter into a greased 10-inch springform pan. Arrange apples on top with ribbed cut edges side up. Cover cake with brown paper. Bake at 350° for 40 minutes. Uncover and bake an additional 10 minutes. Sprinkle cake with remaining sugar. Serve cooled cake with whipped cream.

Apple Cake with Rum Sauce

Elaine Jurkovich, Aurora, Minnesota

1/4 cup butter
1 cup sugar
1 egg
1 cup flour
1/2 teaspoon salt

Rum Sauce:
1/2 cup brown sugar
1/2 cup white sugar

1 teaspoon baking soda
1 teaspoon cinnamon
1 teaspoon vanilla
2 tablespoons hot water
2 1/2 cups peeled and diced apples
1/2 cup chopped nuts

1/4 cup butter
1/2 cup cream
1 tablespoon rum

(continued)

Apple Cake with Rum Sauce *(continued)*

Cream butter and sugar; add egg. Sift together flour, salt, baking soda, and cinnamon. Combine butter and flour mixtures. Add remaining ingredients; mix well. Pour into a greased 9-inch square pan and bake at 350° for 45 minutes.

Rum Sauce: Mix all sauce ingredients except rum in a double boiler and heat. Cook for 2 minutes after heated; remove from heat. Add rum. Serve over cake.

Kuchen

Gladys Haberman, Aurora, Minnesota

Dough:
1 package dry yeast
1/4 cup lukewarm water
1 cup milk
1/4 cup sugar
1 teaspoon salt
4 cups flour, divided
1 egg, beaten
1/4 cup shortening, melted and cooled
2 cups pared chopped apples, for top

Topping:
1 cup water
1/2 cup oil
1/2 cup sugar
2 eggs
3 tablespoons flour
1/2 cup canned milk or cream

(continued)

Kuchen *(continued)*

Dough: Dissolve yeast in lukewarm water and let sit for 5 minutes. Scald milk, let cool and mix in the softened yeast. Add sugar and salt; mix well. Add 2 cups flour and beat 1 minute. Add egg and shortening; mix well. Add another 2 cups flour very gradually and mix. Let sit in a covered dish for 10 minutes. Knead dough until it springs back when pressed with finger. Press into a 9x13-inch baking dish. Let rise until doubled in bulk. Spread with apples and cover with topping. Bake at 350° for 30 minutes.

Topping: Combine water, oil, and sugar and bring to a boil. Combine eggs, flour, and milk; beat together. Add to boiling mixture; boil until thickened.

Yummy Apple Muffins

2 cups flour
1/4 cup sugar
3 teaspoons baking powder
1/2 teaspoon salt
1/2 cup shortening

1 egg, beaten
1 cup milk
1 cup finely chopped apples
1/4 teaspoon cinnamon
1 tablespoon sugar

Combine flour, 1/4 cup sugar, baking powder, and salt. Cut in shortening until mixture resembles coarse meal. Add beaten egg and milk; beat about 30 seconds. Fold in chopped apples. Fill well-greased muffin tins about 2/3 full. Combine cinnamon and 1 tablespoon sugar; sprinkle muffins with mixture. Bake at 400° for 25 t o 30 minutes.

Beverages and Snacks

Camper's Hot Cocoa	57
Hot Spiced Percolator Punch	56
Jerky	59
Russian Tea	55
Scandinavian Egg Coffee	58

Teepee, Mille Lacs Indian Museum

Russian Tea

2 cups orange breakfast drink mix
1/2 cup sugar
1/2 cup instant tea

1 teaspoon cinnamon
1/2 teaspoon cloves
1/2 teaspoon nutmeg
1 5.5-ounce package lemonade mix

Combine all ingredients and store in an airtight container.

To use: Add 2 teaspoons of the mixture to 1 cup of hot water.

Hot Spiced Percolator Punch

You need a 30-cup automatic percolator.

9 cups unsweetened pineapple juice	1 cup brown sugar
9 cups cranberry juice	4 1/2 tablespoons whole cloves
4 1/4 cups water	4 cinnamon sticks, broken
	1/4 teaspoon salt

Combine juices, water, and sugar in percolator. Place spices and salt in the percolator basket. Allow to go through perk cycle.

Note: Do not allow punch to sit in an aluminum container for a long period of time.

Camper's Hot Cocoa

10 cups dry milk
2 cups powdered creamer

3 cups powdered instant chocolate milk mix, such as Quick
1 cup sifted powdered sugar

Combine all ingredients; mix well. Store in an airtight container. Makes enough for about 48 cups.

To use: Add 1/3 cup milk to 1 cup boiling water.

Scandinavian Egg Coffee

5 cups cold water
6 rounded teaspoons coffee

1 1/2 teaspoons egg, slightly beaten
1 teaspoon cold water
2 tablespoons cold water

Bring 5 cups water to a boil. Mix coffee, egg, and 1 teaspoon cold water. Add to boiling water; simmer 3 to 4 minutes. Add 2 tablespoons cold water to settle grounds.

Jerky

1 1/2 pounds venison or beef
1/4 cup soy sauce
1/4 cup Worcestershire sauce
1 teaspoon liquid smoke
1/2 teaspoon garlic powder
1 teaspoon onion powder
1 teaspoon MSG, optional
1/3 teaspoon freshly ground pepper
1/3 teaspoon salt

For easier slicing, place meat in freezer until partially frozen. Cut meat into 1/4-inch pieces across the grain; trim fat. Place strips of meat into a wide-mouth jar. Mix remaining ingredients and pour into jar and cover. Place jar on side in refrigerator for 24 hours, turning jar occasionally. Place meat strips on a paper towel to drain. Put strips on racks over pans; do not bake but dry out by setting the oven to the lowest heat possible and leaving the oven door slightly ajar. Let meat dry out for 10 hours or until it is of the consistency desired.

Soups, Stews, Sauces, and Salads

Ash River Trail Schmooie	68
Elma and Sonia's Beef Mojakka	67
Finnish Pea Soup	61
Fresh Garden Summer Soup	63
Honey Mustard Dressing	72
Meatball Soup	64
Rekola's Beef Mojakka	66
Rhubarb Jam	65
Sauerkraut Salad	73
Spiced Rhubarb	62
Venison Stew	70

Paul Bunyan, Bemidji, Minnesota

Finnish Pea Soup

A traditional meal after a day of sledding.

1 pound whole white or yellow peas	4 cups cubed ham
1/2 pound yellow split peas	2 cups diced carrots
1 ham bone	4 cups cubed potatoes
5 whole allspice	1/4 cup minced onion
5 whole peppercorns	2 stalks celery, diced
1 1/2 gallons water	salt and pepper to taste

Rinse peas well and soak overnight in a generous amount of water. Boil peas, ham bone, allspice, and peppercorns in water for 1 1/2 hours until the skin of the peas loosens. Remove ham bone and scrape meat from bone. Add meat and remaining ingredients to the boiling mixture. Reduce heat and simmer, stirring occasionally, for 1 to 2 hours. Add additional water if soup gets too thick. Serves 10 to 12.

Spiced Rhubarb

12 cups rhubarb, chopped
4 cups sugar
2 cups raspberry vinegar

2 teaspoons ginger
2 teaspoons cinnamon
2 teaspoons ground cloves

In a large kettle, combine all ingredients and bring to a boil. Reduce heat and simmer until rhubarb is transparent. Drain rhubarb, reserving juices. Pack rhubarb into hot sterilized jars, filling the jars 3/4 full. Cook reserved juice over high heat until reduced to a thick syrup. Pour hot syrup over rhubarb to the top of the jars and seal while still hot. Store a few days before using. Makes a tasty accompaniment to roast pork or baked ham.

Fresh Garden Summer Soup

1 medium-sized onion, chopped
2 cups cubed potatoes or
   tiny whole potatoes

3/4 cup sliced carrots
1 cup peas
3 cups milk
3 tablespoons butter or margarine

Boil onion and potatoes in salted water to cover. Reduce heat and simmer about 5 minutes. Add carrots and simmer another 5 minutes. Add peas and simmer until vegetables are done; do not drain. Add milk and butter and bring to a boil. Remove from heat and set aside for 5 minutes before serving. Serves 3 to 4.

Meatball Soup

- 1 quart beef broth
- 1 pound extra-lean ground beef
- 1 egg
- 1 teaspoon salt
- 1/4 teaspoon pepper
- 10 green onions with tops, cut into 1/2-inch pieces
- 1 cup thinly sliced celery
- 1 cup thinly sliced carrots
- 1/2 small head cabbage, shredded
- 2 tomatoes, peeled and cut into eighths
- 1/2 cup uncooked rice
- 1 bay leaf
- 1 teaspoon basil
- 2 to 3 tablespoons soy sauce
- 2 tablespoons minced parsley

In a large pot, simmer broth. Mix ground beef, egg, salt, and pepper. Shape into 1 1/2-inch balls and drop into broth. Add onions, celery, carrots, cabbage, tomatoes, rice, bay leaf, and basil. Simmer, covered, for 35 minutes, stirring occasionally. Discard bay leaf. Stir in soy sauce. Serve garnished with parsley. Serves 6 to 8.

Rhubarb Jam

6 cups rhubarb, diced
4 cups sugar
1 can apricot pie filling

rind of 1 orange, grated
1 3-ounce package orange
    flavored gelatin

In a large saucepan, combine rhubarb and sugar. Let stand overnight. Boil for 10 minutes. Add pie filling and rind; return to a boil. Add gelatin and mix. Pour into sterilized jars and seal while hot. Makes 9 cups.

Rekola's Beef Mojakka

Ironwood USA, Chisholm, Minnesota
This recipe tied for first place in the 1989 Mojakka Cookoff.

1 pound beef short ribs	5 whole allspice
1 tablespoon shortening	3 to 4 black peppercorns
salt to taste	2 medium-sized onions, chopped,
4 cups water	(garden green onions are very good)
1 or 2 beef bouillon cubes	2 medium-sized carrots, chopped
several sprigs parsley	5 medium-sized potatoes, chopped

Brown the meat in the shortening; add salt to taste. Add water and bouillon; bring to a boil. Reduce heat and simmer for about 1/2 hour. Add parsley, allspice, peppercorns, and onions. Simmer until meat is tender, about 1 hour. Remove meat and cut into bite-sized pieces; return to pot and add carrots and potatoes. Cook until vegetables are tender, about 15 to 20 minutes.

Elma and Sonia's Beef Mojakka
Ironworld USA, Chisholm, Minnesota
This recipe tied for first place in the 1989 Mojakka Cookoff.

2 quarts water	1/2 small rutabaga, cut up
1/2 pound beef	1 small onion, cut up
soup bone	2 small carrots, cut up
10 whole allspice	4 medium-sized potatoes, cut up
2 to 3 peppercorns	salt to taste

Bring water to a boil; add beef and soup bone. Cook, skimming pot occasionally. Remove meat when tender. Add allspice, peppercorns, rutabaga, onion, and carrots to pot. Cook for another 30 minutes and add potatoes. Cut meat into bite-sized pieces and return to pot. Simmer until vegetables are tender; season to taste.

Ash River Trail Schmooie

BarBara Luce, Ash River Trail, Orr, Minnesota

BarBara is a member of the citizen's committee on Voyageurs National Park. BarBara writes, "This is actually a chili rather than a stew. It was the creation of a friend Dan and I knew when we were first married. He was a barnstormer and stunt flyer and ran a small parachute-packing business at the old Crystal airport north of Minneapolis."

- 2 pounds ground venison
- 1/4 pound ground pork
- 1 large onion, chopped
- 2 large celery stalks, chopped
- 1 8-ounce can mushroom pieces
- 4 tablespoons chopped parsley
- 1 small can each: red and green peppers, chopped
- chili powder, salt, pepper, paprika, ground sage to taste
- 4 28-ounce cans kidney beans and juice
- 2 28-ounce cans tomatoes, undrained, cut into bite-size pieces

Ash River Trail Schmooie *(continued)*

Garnish:

cheese or sour cream green onions, chopped

Brown venison and pork in a large pot. Add onion, celery and mushrooms. Cook, stirring for about 10 minutes. Add parsley, peppers and seasonings to taste. Cook another 10 minutes. Add beans and tomatoes with liquids. Cook slowly, stirring often for 2 hours. May be served immediately. It is better, however, if cooled and refrigerated for several days and then reheated. Serve each bowl topped with a slice of your choice of cheese or a dollop of sour cream, and sprinkled with green onion. Serves 8 to 10.

Venison Stew
BarBara Luce

2 pounds 1-inch chunks venison
1 cup flour
salt, pepper and paprika, to taste
1 tablespoon butter
1 tablespoon oil
1 large onion, cut into wedges
1 large clove garlic
4 cups boiling water
1 teaspoon lemon juice

1 teaspoon Worcestershire sauce
2 medium-sized bay leaves
1 tablespoon salt
1/2 teaspoon pepper
dash of ground cloves
1 teaspoon salt
4 large carrots, sliced
4 large potatoes, cubed
1 pound frozen green peas

(continued)

Venison Stew *(continued)*

Dumplings:
1 cup flour
1 1/2 teaspoons baking powder
1/2 teaspoon salt
chopped parsley, optional
2 tablespoons oil
1 egg, beaten
1/4 cup plus 2 tablespoons milk

Dredge chunks of venison in flour seasoned with salt, pepper, and paprika. Brown meat in butter and oil, adding more oil if necessary. Add onion and garlic, cooking until limp. Add boiling water, lemon juice, Worcestershire sauce, bay leaves, salt, pepper, cloves, and sugar. Simmer slowly, stirring occasionally for 2 hours. Add carrots and potatoes; cook until they are fork tender. Stir in the frozen peas and simmer until they are cooked through.

Dumplings: Mix dry ingredients and parsley if used. Mix oil, egg, and milk together and add to dry mixture. Mix well and drop by spoonfuls onto simmering stew. Cover tightly and simmer until tops of dumplings are dry to the touch, about 10 to 15 minutes. Serves 6 to 8.

Honey Mustard Dressing

1 egg
1/2 teaspoon salt
2 tablespoons honey
1/2 teaspoon dry mustard
3 tablespoons vinegar, divided
1 small onion, minced
parsley and celery leaves, dry or fresh
1 cup oil

Blend egg, salt, honey, mustard, 1 tablespoon vinegar, onion, and leaves in a blender. Add oil slowly, while blending, until mixture thickens. Add remaining vinegar and blend.

Sauerkraut Salad

1/2 cup sugar
1/2 cup vinegar
1 16-ounce can sauerkraut,
   undrained

1 cup diced celery
1 cup diced green pepper
1 small onion, chopped
1/4 cup pimiento, drained
   and chopped

Heat sugar and vinegar until sugar is dissolved. Cool vinegar mixture and add remaining ingredients. Chill and serve as a salad or in a Polish sausage sandwich.

Breads

Finnish Flat Bread	75
Homemade Snack Crackers	83
Horns	81
Norwegian Lefse	80
Potica Coffeecake	77
Raised Doughnuts	82
Swedish Rye Bread	79

Loon, Minnesota state bird

Finnish Flat Bread

4 cups lukewarm water
2 tablespoons sugar
2 packages dry yeast
2 teaspoons salt
1/4 cup oil or melted shortening

1 cup oat bran
2 cups cracked wheat
1/2 cup wheat germ
6 cups white flour as needed to make a stiff dough
melted butter

Combine water, sugar, yeast, salt, and oil; set aside until the yeast begins to bubble. Add oat bran, cracked wheat, wheat germ, and enough white flour to make a sticky, but somewhat stiff dough. On a floured surface, knead dough until it is no longer sticky. Place dough in a greased bowl and turn to coat. Cover and let rise until double in bulk, about 1 hour.

(continued)

Finnish Flat Bread   *(continued)*

Punch dough down and divide into four parts. Let rest for 10 minutes and form into round loaves. Place loaves on a cookie sheet and flatten slightly, let rise again for 15 minutes, flatten again and poke holes in each loaf with a fork. Bake at 375° until bottoms of loaves are firm, about 15 to 25 minutes. Slide off cookie sheet and bake on oven rack for an additional 15 minutes. Turn loaves around in oven and bake an additional 15 to 20 minutes or until loaves are nicely browned. Remove from oven and brush with melted butter.

Note: The last flour used should be added gradually to keep dough from being too stiff. Gerry does this with all her baking because: "Every flour is different."

Potica Coffeecake

A Slovak favorite.

2 packages dry yeast
1/3 cup warm water
1/2 cup scalded milk
3/4 cup butter or margarine

Filling:
1/3 cup milk
1 1/2 cups ground walnuts
2 tablespoons brown sugar

Glaze:
3/4 cup powdered sugar

1/2 teaspoon salt
3 tablespoons sugar
3 egg yolks, beaten
2 1/2 to 2 3/4 cups flour

2 tablespoons honey
1 teaspoon vanilla or cinnamon
3 egg whites
3/4 cup sugar

2 tablespoons frozen orange
  juice concentrate
1 teaspoon water

(continued)

Potica Coffeecake *(continued)*

Cake: Dissolve yeast in warm water. Scald milk and add butter. Add salt and sugar; set aside to cool to lukewarm. Stir egg yolks into milk mixture. Pour into a large mixing bowl and gradually add flour and yeast mixture. Beat until well blended. Cover and refrigerate overnight.

Filling: Heat milk until very hot. Combine nuts and brown sugar. Add honey and cinnamon to milk mixture; pour over nut mixture; cool. Beat egg whites, gradually adding sugar, until soft peaks are formed. Fold egg white mixture into nut mixture.

Assembly: Roll out half the dough into an 18x20-inch rectangle on a well-floured pastry cloth. Spread with half the filling. Roll like a jelly roll, starting with the wide end. Place the roll, rolled edge down, into a 10-inch, well-greased, tube pan. Repeat with the second half of the dough, placing the second roll on top of the first. Bake at 350° for 1 hour and 5 minutes. Cool 20 minutes before removing from pan. Drizzle with glaze.

Glaze: Blend all ingredients together well and drizzle over top of cake.

Swedish Rye Bread

Mr. Laurie Lehtinen, Aurora, Minnesota

- 2 cups boiling water
- 2/3 cup brown sugar
- 1/2 cup molasses
- 1 cup shortening
- 4 teaspoons salt
- 1 quart buttermilk
- 1 teaspoon baking soda
- 5 cups rye flour
- 2 packages dry yeast dissolved in 1/4 cup warm water
- 5 cups white flour

Combine boiling water, sugar, molasses, shortening, and salt; bring to a boil. Remove from heat and pour into a large bowl. Add buttermilk, baking soda, and rye flour; mix. Cool to lukewarm and add yeast and enough white flour to make a stiff dough. Knead dough on a floured surface until dough is smooth and elastic. Let rise until dough is doubled in bulk, about 1 hour. Punch down and shape into 3 loaves. Place into greased and floured 9x5-inch pans. Let rise again until almost double in bulk, 1 hour. Bake at 350° for 1 hour or until done.

Norwegian Lefse

5 well-packed cups of cooked, riced potatoes
1/2 cup margarine
3 tablespoons powdered sugar
2 cups flour
1 teaspoon salt

Add margarine to potatoes while they are still warm. Cool to room temperature. Add powdered sugar, flour, and salt. Knead well and then roll into a log. Cut and measure into 1/3 cup portions, make a round ball of each. On a floured lefse "board"* press each dough ball down and then, using a pastry sleeve and rolling pin, roll into 14-inch circles to fit a lefse griddle*. The secret to making lefse is the use of the lefse stick*. For the last roll across the dough use a grooved lefse rolling pin, which marks the dough and makes it thinner. Grill dough on a lefse griddle for about 1 to 2 minutes on each side. Fold each lefse in half or quarters. Cool between paper towels and store in plastic bags.
*Found in specialty and culinary shops.

Horns

Elaine Jurkovich, Aurora, Minnesota

Dough:
1 package dry yeast
1/2 cup lukewarm water
4 cups flour
1 pound butter
4 egg yolks, unbeaten

Filling:
1 pound walnuts, ground
1 cup sugar
6 egg whites, stiffly beaten

Dough: Dissolve yeast in milk. Cut butter into flour until mixture resembles meal. Combine milk mixture and egg yolks with flour mixture, mixing until dough is soft and sticky.

Filling: Combine nuts and sugar. Add stiffly beaten egg whites; mix.

Assembly: Take a baseball-sized piece of dough and roll very thin, as you would for an 8-inch pie crust. Cover circle with filling and cut circle into wedges. Roll into crescent shapes. Repeat until all dough and filling is used. Place on greased cookie sheets. Bake at 350° for 30 minutes.

Raised Doughnuts

These used to be a lumberjack's delight.

1 1/2 cups milk	1 cup warm water
2/3 cup shortening	4 eggs
2 teaspoons salt	1/2 cup sugar
2 packages dry yeast	7 cups flour, divided
	oil for frying

Scald milk and add shortening and salt; cool. Dissolve yeast in warm water; set aside until bubbly. Beat eggs with sugar and blend with milk and yeast mixtures. Stir in flour 1 cup at a time until half of the flour is used. Place remaining flour on board and knead into dough. Cover the dough and let rise in a warm place for 1 hour. Turn out on a floured board and roll to 3/4 inch thick; cut with a doughnut cutter. Cover and let rise 1 hour. Fry in 365° oil with the raised side down until golden. Makes 5 dozen doughnuts.

Homemade Snack Crackers

BarBara Luce

2 1/2 cups shredded Cheddar cheese
1/2 cup soft butter
1/4 cup milk
1 teaspoon prepared mustard
3/4 cup flour
3/4 cup cornmeal
toasted sesame or poppy seeds

Beat together cheese, butter, milk, and mustard until well blended. Add flour and cornmeal and mix well. Divide in 2 and shape each half into a log 8 inches long. Wrap tightly in plastic wrap and refrigerate for 2 hours. Slice logs into 1/8-inch slices and place on greased cookie sheets. Sprinkle with seeds. Bake at 375° for 10 minutes or until edges of crackers are golden brown. Cool on a rack and store in loosely covered containers. If necessary to crisp before serving, bake on an ungreased sheet at 350° for 3 to 4 minutes, watching carefully.

Fish, Meat, Poultry, and Wild Game

Fish:
Baked Lutefisk	115
Baked Stuffed Lake Superior Trout	116
Barbecued Smelt	108
Batter for Fried Walleye	113
Boundary Waters Walleye	112
Buttered-Poached Walleye	110
Campfire Smelt	107
Cocktail Walleye	111
Fresh Fish Chowder	109
Lutefisk	115
Minnesota Lobster	114
Pickled Fish	118

Poultry:
Creamed Partridge	101
Minnesota Roasted Pheasant	106
Northern Minnesota Partridge Pie	102
Oven Fried Chicken	105
Wild Duck Rae's Way	103
Turkey Loaf	104

Meat and Wild Game:
Campfire Supper	100
Cabbage Casserole	95
Cabbage Rolls	92
Egg Rolls	93
Finnish Cabbage Rolls	90
Ham Loaf with Jelly Sauce	85
Hungry Boy Casserole	96
Iron Miners' Pasty	98
Marinade for Venison Steak	86
Swedish Kalops	89
Swedish Meatballs	88
Viking Bar-B-Ques	87

Ham Loaf with Jelly Sauce

Cynthia Baker, Aurora

Ham Loaf:
2 pounds ground ham
1 pound ground pork
1 egg
1 cup bread or cracker crumbs

Jelly Sauce:
1 teaspoon dry mustard
1/4 teaspoon ground cloves

1/2 cup milk
3 tablespoons condensed tomato soup
1/2 teaspoon paprika
1/4 teaspoon salt
1 medium-sized onion, sliced

1/4 teaspoon cinnamon
2 tablespoons vinegar
1 6-ounce jar apple jelly

Ham Loaf: Mix all ingredients except onion together and shape into a loaf. Place in a loaf pan. Place onion slices over top. Bake at 350° for 1 1/2 hours.

Jelly Sauce: Mix all ingredients together and heat over low heat until jelly melts into small chunks. Serve over ham loaf. Serves 6 to 8.

Marinade for Venison Steak

2 cloves garlic, minced
1/4 cup vinegar
1/4 cup soy sauce

1 tablespoon Worcestershire sauce
1 teaspoon oil
1/2 cup water

Blend all ingredients thoroughly. Use to marinate venison.

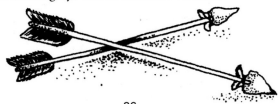

Viking Bar-B-Ques

Lucille Niemi, Aurora, Minnesota

A crowd pleaser on Super Bowl Sunday.

1 6-pound beef roast
1 quart ginger ale
1 28-ounce bottle ketchup
18 to 24 buns

Combine all ingredients except buns in a roaster. Cover and bake at 300° for 6 hours or until beef shreds with a fork. Mix sauce and meat together and serve on buns.

Viking ship head, Heritage Hjemkømst Center, Moorhead, Minnesota

Swedish Meatballs

2 tablespoons bread or cracker crumbs
1/3 pound ground pork
2/3 pound ground beef
2 boiled, cold potatoes, mashed

2 tablespoons milk
1 small onion, grated
1 teaspoon salt
pepper to taste
nutmeg, optional
1/2 cup flour

Combine crumbs, meat, potatoes, milk, onion, salt, pepper, and nutmeg; mix well and shape into balls. Roll in flour and place in a greased baking dish. Bake, uncovered, at 375° for 1 hour. Serves 4.

Swedish Kalops
Ironworld USA, Chisholm, Minnesota

1 pound beef steak, cut into
   1-inch cubes
1/2 cup flour
salt and pepper to taste
1 tablespoon oil
1 1/2 cups water
3 whole allspice
1 small onion, chopped

Dredge beef in flour and season to taste. In a Dutch oven, brown beef in oil. Add water, allspice, and onion; simmer for 1 hour. Serve over hot mashed potatoes. Serves 4.

Finnish Cabbage Rolls

1 2 1/2- to 3-pound head cabbage
1/2 cup margarine, divided
1 cup finely chopped onion
1 pound ground beef
1 cup milk
1 egg, slightly beaten
1 cup cooked rice
1/2 teaspoon salt
1/2 teaspoon ground allspice
1/4 teaspoon pepper
1/2 cup dark corn syrup

Core cabbage; hold under running water to remove 12 large leaves, allowing water to fill space between leaf and head for easy removal. Cook leaves and remaining head in boiling salted water for 7 to 10 minutes or until almost tender; drain and cool. Set aside the separate leaves and chop the remaining head of cabbage to yield 2 cups.

(continued)

Finnish Cabbage Rolls   *(continued)*

Sauté onion in 1/4 cup margarine until golden brown. Remove from heat and stir in the beef, chopped cabbage, milk, egg, rice, salt, allspice, and pepper. Place about 1/3 cup of the meat mixture into the center of each cabbage leaf. Wrap leaf around the filling and tuck ends in. Place seam side down in 9x13-inch baking dish. Melt remaining margarine; brush rolls with margarine. Pour corn syrup over cabbage rolls and bake at 400° for 1 hour, turning once. Reduce heat to 350°. Turn rolls seam side down again and bake 30 additional minutes or until well glazed and browned. Serves 6.

Cabbage Rolls

An Iron Range favorite for celebrations.

- 3/4 cup uncooked rice
- 2 pounds ground ham
- 1 1/2 pounds ground pork
- 1 pound ground beef
- 1 teaspoon salt
- 1/2 teaspoon pepper
- 6 cloves garlic, minced
- 2 eggs
- 1 small onion, chopped fine
- 1 cup tomato sauce
- 1 large cabbage
- 2 27-ounce cans sauerkraut
- 1 quart water

Combine rice, meat, salt, pepper, garlic, eggs, onion, and tomato sauce. Roll into egg-sized balls. Soak cabbage leaves in hot water until you are able to remove softened leaves. Place meatball in the center of each leaf. Fold closed and secure with a toothpick. Cover bottom of kettle with sauerkraut. Add a layer of cabbage rolls; cover with sauerkraut. Repeat until all cabbage rolls are used. Cover with sauerkraut and add water. Simmer for 2 1/2 hours.

Egg Rolls
Elaine Popovich, Aurora, Minnesota

2 whole chicken breasts, skinned
2 pounds ground pork
salt, pepper, and soy sauce to taste
cooking oil
2 stalks Chinese celery, chopped
1 medium-sized Chinese cabbage, chopped
1 medium-sized cabbage, chopped
2 to 3 bunches green onion, chopped
1 teaspoon MSG, optional
2 tablespoons peanut butter
3 packages egg roll wraps
1 egg, beaten

Cook chicken breasts with salt and pepper until done; set aside to cool. Brown pork with salt, pepper, and soy sauce until cooked through. In a wok or large kettle, stir-fry Chinese celery in about 2 tablespoons of cooking oil for 3 to 5 minutes.

(continued)

Egg Rolls   *(continued)*

Add both cabbages and green onions; stir-fry an additional 3 to 5 minutes or until vegetables are crisp tender; add additional oil if needed. Chop chicken and add to vegetables with pork. Season to taste and add MSG if desired and peanut butter. Mix well and place in a colander. Place egg roll wrapper flour side up; brush edges with egg. Put 2 tablespoons meat mixture in corner of wrap, fold corner over first and then the sides toward the middle. Brush sides with egg and roll toward the other corner. Seal tightly. Fry in 350° oil for about 3 minutes or until lightly browned. Drain on paper towels. Makes about 25 to 30.

Note: Fried rolls freeze well. To reheat place on a cookie sheet and bake at 350° for 15 to 20 minutes or in a microwave for about 1 minute. If skins are too soft after baking re-fry the rolls in about 2 tablespoons of cooking oil.

Cabbage Casserole

1 pound ground beef
1 medium-sized onion, chopped
1 teaspoon salt

1 small cabbage
1 10 3/4-ounce can tomato soup
1 cup water
1/2 cup uncooked rice

Brown ground beef with onion; add salt. Cut cabbage into 1-inch cubes; place into a greased 3-quart casserole. Pour beef mixture over cabbage. Combine tomato soup, water, and rice; add to casserole. Bake, covered, at 350° for 1 1/2 hours. Stir before serving. Serves 6.

Hungry Boy Casserole
BarBara Luce

2 pounds ground venison
1/4 pound ground pork
1 cup chopped celery
1/2 cup chopped onion
1 large green pepper, chopped

1 large clove garlic, chopped
1 6-ounce can tomato paste
salt and pepper to taste
1 teaspoon paprika
1-pound can pork and beans
1-pound can navy beans

Filling:
1/2 cup sliced pimiento stuffed olives

1/4 cup sliced toasted almonds

Dough:
1 1/2 cups flour
2 teaspoons baking powder

1/2 teaspoon salt
1/4 cup cold butter
1/2 cup milk

(continued)

Hungry Boy Casserole   *(continued)*

In a Dutch oven, brown meats lightly. Add vegetables and garlic and sauté lightly. Stir in tomato paste. Remove 1 cup of this mixture and reserve. Add seasonings and beans to Dutch oven and keep warm.

Filling: Add olives and almonds to reserved mixture; blend.

Dough: Combine flour, baking powder, and salt. Cut in cold butter until crumbly; add milk and mix well. Turn onto a lightly floured board and knead lightly. Roll into a 10x18-inch rectangle. Spread with reserved mixture and roll jellyroll fashion from the wide end. Seal edges by pinching. Place seam-side down and cut into equal slices, about 16 pieces, with a serrated, floured knife. Place on top of the bean-meat mixture and bake at 425° for 25 to 30 minutes until mixture is bubbly and rolls are browned. Serves 8.

Iron Miners' Pasty

Cornish miners introduced pasties to the Range.

Pasty Dough:

1 teaspoon salt
3 cups flour
1 cup shortening

1 egg
1 tablespoon vinegar
water

Filling:

6 cups cubed potatoes
2 cups cubed carrots
2 cups cubed rutabaga

2 tablespoons instant chopped onion,
    or 1/4 cup fresh minced onion
1 1/2 pounds coarsely ground beef
1 teaspoon salt
pepper to taste

(continued)

Iron Miners' Pastry *(continued)*

Pasty Dough: Combine salt and flour; cut in shortening. Place egg and vinegar into a measuring cup; add water to fill to 1 cup. Blend dry and liquid ingredients until a soft dough is formed. Add additional flour if dough is too soft. Divide dough into 6 parts and roll into six individual circles.

Filling: Combine vegetables and beef; season to taste. Divide filling onto the six circles, placing the filling on half of each circle. Brush the edge of each circle with water and fold half the circle over the filling. Crimp the edges to seal well. Do not prick. Place on an ungreased baking sheet and bake at 375° for 1 hour.

Campfire Supper

Sauce:
1/2 cup vinegar
1/2 cup ketchup
2 tablespoons Worcestershire sauce

2 tablespoons melted butter
1 teaspoon prepared mustard
juice of 1 lemon
salt and pepper

2 pounds ground beef
salt and pepper
1 medium-sized onion, sliced
2 carrots, cut into strips

1 medium-sized potato, sliced lengthwise
2 stalks celery, cut into 3-inch lengths

Sauce: Blend sauce ingredients together. Cut 6 squares of heavy-duty aluminum foil. Shape beef into 6 patties. Place each patty onto the center of a foil piece. Cover each patty with onion, carrot strips, potato slices, and celery sticks. Divide the sauce between the patties. Seal the foil pouches tightly. Place 4 inches from hot coals for about 30 minutes or until done.

Creamed Partridge

3 to 4 partridges
1 10 3/4-ounce can cream of mushroom soup
1 10 3/4-ounce can cream of chicken soup
1/2 cup water
1/2 cup milk
1 medium-sized onion, diced
salt and pepper
1 8-ounce can mushrooms

Place partridges in a large pot and cover with about 2 cups water. Cover and steam for 30 minutes or until partridges are tender. Remove meat from bones and mix with remaining ingredients. Cook for about 15 minutes at medium heat, stirring occasionally. Serve over mashed potatoes. Serves 6.

Northern Minnesota Partridge Pie

Ironworld USA, Chisholm, Minnesota

- 6 strips bacon
- 3 partridges, grouse or quail
- 3 cups sherry
- 3 potatoes, diced
- 1 onion, diced
- 2 carrots, diced
- 1 teaspoons salt
- 1/4 teaspoon pepper
- 1/8 teaspoon sage
- 1 clove garlic, minced
- pastry for 1 10-inch pie crust

Wrap bacon around partridges and simmer in sherry over medium heat for 45 minutes or until tender. Remove meat from bones and dice. Dice bacon. Combine vegetables, seasonings, and meat; mix well. Pour into a greased 10-inch pie pan and cover with the pastry. Pierce with fork. Bake at 350° for 1 hour and 45 minutes. Serves 8.

Wild Duck Rae's Way

Mrs. Alan Burchell, Moosehorn Resort, Lake Kabetogama, Ray, Minnesota

1 wild duck, skin on and
   well cleaned
seasoned tenderizer
1 slice of dry bread, crumbled
giblets, cut up, optional

1/2 stalk celery, sliced
1/2 cup chopped onion
poultry seasoning
salt and pepper
hot water or broth to moisten

Sprinkle inside of duck with seasoned tenderizer. Prepare stuffing by tossing together bread, giblets, celery, onion and seasonings; moisten with hot water and broth. Pack loosely into bird and place in a pan. (Loaf pan for 1 duck, 8-inch square for 2.) Prop open end of bird up with crushed foil, to keep fat from drenching the stuffing. Cover pan with foil. Roast at 325° for 2 to 3 hours, depending on size of bird. Remove from oven; drain off fat. Return to oven uncovered for 1/2 hour or until the skin is crisp.

Turkey Loaf

1 medium-sized carrot
1 medium-sized potato
2 tablespoons minced onion
2 slices bread

2 pounds ground turkey
1/4 cup milk
1 teaspoon salt
pepper to taste

Place carrot, potato and onion into a food processor and chop fine. Add bread and process. Mix together all ingredients. Place into a loaf pan. Bake at 350° for about 1 hour. Serves 6 to 8.

Oven Fried Chicken

1 cup flour
2 teaspoons salt
1 teaspoon coarsely ground pepper
1/2 teaspoon garlic salt

1/4 teaspoon nutmeg
1/4 teaspoon oregano
2 1/2 to 3 pounds chicken pieces
1/4 teaspoon paprika
1 stick margarine, melted

In a large plastic bag, combine flour and seasonings. Wash chicken and pat dry. Using 2 or 3 pieces of chicken at a time, shake in the seasoning mix; continue until all the chicken pieces are coated. Pour the margarine into a jellyroll pan. Place coated chicken pieces in pan. Bake at 400° for 1/2 hour; turn pieces and bake an additional 1/2 hour. Serves 6.

Minnesota Roast Pheasant

1 pheasant, cut into serving-sized
  pieces
3/4 cup flour
1 teaspoon salt
1/4 teaspoon pepper
1/2 cup boiling water
1 cup sweet or sour cream
white cooking wine, optional

Dredge pheasant in flour and season with salt and pepper. Brown pheasant in hot oil. Arrange pheasant in a greased casserole and add cream. Bake uncovered at 325° for 1 hour or until tender. Add water as needed and baste occasionally with cream and drippings. Add a small amount of white wine the last 30 minutes of baking to tenderize and add flavor.

Campfire Smelt

3 pounds dressed smelt	1/3 cup chopped onion
salt and pepper	1/3 cup chopped parsley
	3 strips bacon, cut in half

Wash smelt and pat dry. Cut 6 pieces of heavy-duty aluminum foil, 12x12-inches each and grease lightly. Divide fish into 6 portions and place on foil pieces. Season each to taste. Divide onion and parsley among the portions and top each with a half strip of bacon. Fold the foil together to seal the fish, using double folds to close. Place packages on a grill about 4 inches from the hot coals. Cook for 10 to 15 minutes or until fish flakes.

Barbecued Smelt

1/4 cup chopped onion
2 1/2 tablespoons finely chopped
   green pepper
1 clove garlic, minced

2 1/2 tablespoons butter
1 tablespoon tomato sauce
1 tablespoon sugar
1/4 teaspoon pepper
2 pounds dressed smelt

Sauté onion, green pepper, and garlic in the butter. Add tomato sauce, sugar, and pepper; simmer for 5 minutes. Remove from heat and cool. Marinate fish in sauce for 45 minutes, turning once. Place fish on a broiling rack and broil for 5 to 10 minutes, basting with sauce. Turn fish and broil until the fish flakes easily. Serves 6.

Fresh Fish Chowder

2 to 3 medium-sized potatoes,
    peeled and quartered
1 medium-sized onion, quartered
1 teaspoon salt
3 whole allspice
3 whole peppercorns

1 cup water
1/2 pound fish fillets
1 tablespoon flour
1 tablespoon melted butter
1/4 cup milk
1 cup evaporated milk
chopped dill and parsley

Boil potatoes, onion, and seasoning in 1 cup of water or enough to cover, until tender, about 10 minutes. Reduce heat to a simmer and lay fish on top. Cover and simmer until fish flakes easily, about 10 minutes. Stir flour into melted butter until smooth. Add 1/4 cup milk and stir gently. Pour flour mixture and evaporated milk over fish and heat until slightly thickened. Pour into 2 serving bowls and garnish with dill and parsley.

Butter-Poached Walleye

1 2- to 3-pound walleye, filleted
1/2 cup water
1/4 pound butter, softened
1 medium-sized onion, sliced
1 tablespoon lemon juice
1 teaspoon dried dill weed
salt and pepper to taste

Place fillets side by side in a casserole with a tight fitting lid; add water. Dot with butter. Cover fillets with onion slices. Drizzle lemon juice over all. Sprinkle evenly with dill weed, salt, and pepper. Bake, covered, at 350° for 30 minutes or until fish flakes easily. Serves 4.

Cocktail Walleye
BarBara Luce

1 teaspoon lemon juice   3 pounds walleye fillets

Sauce:
2 cups ketchup   1 tablespoon Worcestershire sauce
1 cup chili sauce   1 tablespoon lemon juice
several drops Tabasco sauce   2 tablespoon horseradish, or to taste

Bring lightly salted water to a boil. Add lemon juice. Cut fillets into bite-sized pieces and place in a fry basket or strainer; lower into the boiling water and cook until translucent. Plunge immediately into ice water to cool, then drain thoroughly.
Sauce: Mix ingredients well. In a glass jar, layer sauce and cooked fish, beginning and ending with sauce. Refrigerate for at least 3 days. Serve on crisp crackers. Makes 4 cups.

Boundary Waters Walleye
Donna Patton, Eveleth, Minnesota

2 to 3 pounds walleye fillets
salt and pepper

1/3 cup butter
1 teaspoon honey
paprika

Rinse fillets well and pat dry. Season with salt and pepper. Melt butter with honey. Dip fillets in honey-butter mixture. Place on a broiler pan and broil for about 3 minutes on each side, brushing with honey-butter mixture occasionally. Sprinkle with paprika and serve. Serves 4 to 6.

Batter for Fried Walleye

BarBara Luce

2/3 cup whole-wheat flour
1/3 cup cornstarch
1 teaspoon baking powder
1/2 teaspoon salt
1 egg, beaten
ice water

Combine dry ingredients; add egg and 2/3 cup water or enough to make batter the proper consistency.

Walleye, Minnesota state fish

Minnesota Lobster

3 quarts water
1 medium-sized onion, quartered
salt to taste
1/2 cup lemon juice
3 stalks celery, chopped
3 to 4 pounds fish fillets,
    cut into 2-inch pieces
1 cup butter, melted, divided
paprika

Place water, onion, salt, lemon juice, and celery in a 4-quart pot; bring to a boil. Add fish and boil for 5 minutes. Drain fish and place on a baking sheet. Brush with melted butter and sprinkle with paprika. Broil fish for 2 minutes. Sprinkle with paprika and serve with remaining melted butter. Serves 8.

Note: Northern Pike, Lake Trout, Coho Salmon, Steelhead or any other firm deep-water fish may be used.

Lutefisk

2 pounds lutefisk   1/2 pound butter

Rinse fish thoroughly in cold water. Cut into serving-sized pieces. Wrap fish in cheesecloth and place in cool salted water. Bring water to boil. Cook for 10 minutes or until tender and translucent. Remove and serve with generous amounts of melted butter. Serves 4.

Baked Lutefisk

2 pounds lutefisk   salt
                                     1/2 pound melted butter

Place lutefisk in a greased glass baking dish. Sprinkle with salt and cover with foil. Bake at 350° for 30 to 40 minutes. Serve with melted butter.

Baked Stuffed Lake Superior Trout

1 3- to 4-pound trout, head removed

Green Pepper Stuffing:
1/4 cup butter
1/4 cup chopped onion
1/4 cup chopped green pepper

Parmesan Cheese Stuffing:
2 tablespoons butter
1/4 cup chopped onion

2 teaspoons seasoned salt
1/4 cup butter
green pepper or Parmesan stuffing

1/4 cup sliced water chestnuts
2 cups soft bread crumbs
salt and pepper to taste

2 cups bread crumbs
1/4 cup Parmesan cheese
1/2 teaspoon dried dill
salt and pepper to taste

(continued)

Baked Stuffed Lake Superior Trout   *(continued)*

Clean fish, wash, and pat dry. Sprinkle inside and out with seasoned salt. Make desired stuffing. Stuff fish and close with skewers. Brush with butter and bake at 375° for 30 to 40 minutes or until fish flakes easily.

Green Pepper Stuffing: Sauté onion, green pepper, and water chestnuts in butter until soft. Mix with the bread crumbs and season to taste.

Parmesan Cheese Stuffing: Sauté onion and celery in butter until soft. Mix all ingredients together.

Pickled Fish

pickling salt
water
6 northern pike, about 3 pounds each, filleted and cut into bite-sized pieces

white vinegar to cover fish
4 cups sugar
4 cups white vinegar
1/3 cup pickling spices
2 large onions, sliced
2 cups white wine

In a large pot, place enough water to cover the fish. Make a salt brine by dissolving pickling salt in the water until the mixture is salty enough to float an unbroken egg. Add fish and set aside for 48 hours. Drain and wash fish 4 times in cold water. Return fish to empty pot and cover with vinegar. Set aside for 24 hours. Drain fish; pack into about 8 sterilized quart jars. Combine remaining ingredients and bring to a boil. Remove from heat and cool. Pour the mixture over the fish, and refrigerate.

Vegetables and Side Dishes

Baked Buttercup Squash	125
Carrot Loaf	123
Corn Stuffing Balls	120
Finnish Rutabaga Loaf	122
Jewish Potato Pancakes	128
Kugula	127
Marinated Carrots and Broccoli	126
North Country Fresh Mushroom Pâté	124
Stuffed Squash	121

*Morel mushrooms
Minnesosta state fungus*

Corn Stuffing Balls

1/2 cup chopped onion
1/2 cup chopped celery
4 tablespoons margarine
1 can cream-style corn
1/2 cup water

1 teaspoon poultry seasoning
1/8 teaspoon pepper
1 8-ounce package herb-seasoned stuffing mix
3 eggs, beaten
1/2 cup melted margarine

Sauté onion and celery in 4 tablespoons margarine until tender. Add corn, water, poultry seasoning, and pepper; bring to a boil. Pour over stuffing mix and toss lightly. Stir in eggs. Shape into 9 balls and place in 9x9x2-inch pan. Pour the melted margarine over the balls. Refrigerate until ready to use. Bake at 350° for 35 minutes. Delicious with chicken or pork. Serves 6.

Stuffed Squash

3 medium-sized acorn squash
2 cups coarsely chopped onion
3 tablespoons butter
1 4-ounce can mushrooms

2 tablespoons chopped parsley
salt and pepper, to taste
1 cup shredded cheese
1 tablespoon buttered
corn flake crumbs

Cut squash in half lengthwise; remove seeds and bake, cut side down, at 350° for 35 to 40 minutes or until almost tender. Sauté onion in butter until almost tender. Add mushrooms and parsley. Turn squash, cut side up, and season with salt and pepper. Fill with onion mixture. Bake 15 to 20 minutes longer or until squash is done. Sprinkle top with cheese and crumbs and return to oven to melt cheese. Serves 6.

Finnish Rutabaga Loaf
Ironworld USA, Chisholm, Minnesota

1 medium-sized rutabaga
2 tablespoons butter
2 tablespoons brown sugar
1/2 teaspoon salt
2 tablespoons Cream of Wheat
1 egg, well beaten
1/2 cup cream
cinnamon
butter for top

Pare, slice, and cook rutabaga in water until tender; drain. Mash rutabaga and add butter, sugar, salt, Cream of Wheat, egg, and cream. Mix well and pour into a buttered loaf pan. Sprinkle with cinnamon and dot with butter. Bake at 350° for 35 to 40 minutes. Serves 3.

Carrot Loaf

2 pounds carrots, thinly sliced
4 eggs, beaten
1 1/2 teaspoons sugar

1/2 teaspoon salt
1 tablespoon melted butter
1 1/2 teaspoons cornstarch
2 cups cream

Cover carrots with water and cook until tender. Drain and cool carrots; put through a sieve. Add eggs, sugar, salt, and melted butter. Make a paste of cornstarch and a little cold water; stir into mixture. Mix in the cream. Pour into a loaf pan and bake at 350° for 45 minutes, or until a knife comes out clean. Serves 6.

North Country Fresh Mushroom Pâté

BarBara Luce

1 large green onion, minced
1/2 pound mushrooms, wild or commercial, finely chopped
4 tablespoons melted butter, divided
1/2 teaspoon lemon juice
1/4 cup finely chopped toasted hazelnuts or almonds
1/2 tablespoon Tabasco sauce
2 1/2 teaspoons soy sauce

Sauté onion and mushrooms in 2 tablespoons butter until all liquid is absorbed, about 15 minutes. Chill. Add lemon juice, nuts, Tabasco sauce, soy sauce, and remaining melted butter; blend well. Serve at room temperature. Serves 3.

Baked Buttercup Squash

1 large buttercup squash
2 tablespoons brown sugar
1/2 cup milk

1 tablespoon butter
1 teaspoon salt
1/2 pound bacon, cooked crisp
and crumbled

Cut squash in half lengthwise. Clean out seeds and bake squash at 350° until soft, about 1 1/2 hours. Scoop squash out and mash. Combine brown sugar, milk, butter, and salt. Mix into squash and put squash back into shell. Top with bacon. Serve hot. Serves 4.

Marinated Carrots and Broccoli

1/4 cup water
1 teaspoon salt
2 cups peeled and sliced carrots

2 cups broccoli florets
3 tablespoons vegetable oil
1 tablespoon cider vinegar
1/2 teaspoon dried basil leaves

In a saucepan over moderate heat, boil water with salt. Add carrots and cook, covered, for 5 minutes. Add broccoli and cook an additional 5 minutes. Drain and toss with oil and vinegar. Sprinkle with basil and serve hot. Serves 4.

Kugula

Ironworld USA, Chisholm, Minnesota

6 to 8 medium-sized potatoes
5 pieces bacon, cooked and crumbled
1/4 cup bacon fat
2 eggs
1 teaspoon grated onion
2 tablespoons flour
salt and pepper
sour cream

Peel and grate potatoes. Combine all ingredients except sour cream and place into a shallow casserole that has been greased with bacon fat. Bake at 350° for 50 to 60 minutes. Serve with sour cream. Serves 6 to 8.

Jewish Potato Pancakes

6 medium-sized potatoes
1 small onion, optional
2 eggs, slightly beaten
1/2 teaspoon baking powder
3 tablespoons flour
1/4 teaspoon pepper
1 teaspoon salt
apples, sugar or sour cream for topping

Peel and grate potatoes and onion, if used. Place in a colander and drain for 10 minutes. Combine all ingredients and drop by spoonfuls onto a hot well-greased skillet. Brown on both sides. Place on absorbent paper to drain. Serve with apples, sugar or sour cream. Serves 6.

Variation: For potato cupcakes place the potato mixture in well-greased custard cups and bake at 350° for 40 minutes or until brown.

Desserts and Cookies

Cranberry Cake with Butter Sauce	131	Sunflower Seed Cookies	141
Czech Poppyseed Coffeecake	139	Trail Bars	140
Fruit Soup	130		
Passover Cheesecake	133		
Norwegian Rosettes	143		
Oat Health Bars	142		
Raspberry Crisp	132		
Rhubarb Cake	137		
Rhubarb Cream Pie	138		
Rhubarb Whip	136		
Slovenian Noodle Strudel	135		

Showy Pink and White Lady's Slipper, Minnesota state flower

Fruit Soup
Ironworld USA, Chisholm, Minnesota

1 pound mixed dried fruit
10 cups water
1 cup sugar
1 cinnamon stick
2 tablespoons cornstarch or potato flour
2 tablespoons cold water

Simmer the dried fruit in 10 cups water with sugar and cinnamon until fruit is tender, about 1 hour. Combine the cornstarch and cold water. Bring the soup to a boil and stir in the cornstarch mixture. Cook until clear. Cover and let cool. Serves 12.

Cranberry Cake with Butter Sauce

2 cups flour
1 1/2 cups sugar
2 teaspoons baking powder

Sauce:
1/2 cup butter
1/2 cup brown sugar

2 tablespoons butter, softened
1 cup milk
2 cups cut-up cranberries

1/2 cup sugar
1/2 cup cream
1 teaspoon vanilla

Mix flour, sugar, and baking powder. Add butter, milk, and cranberries; blend. Pour into a greased 9x13-inch pan and bake at 375° for 30 minutes.
Sauce: Heat butter and sugars, but do not boil. Remove from heat and add cream and vanilla. Serve over cake.

Raspberry Crisp

4 cups fresh raspberries
1/3 cup granulated sugar
1/4 cup butter

1/3 cup flour
1/3 cup brown sugar
3/4 cup quick oatmeal

Place berries on bottom of a greased, 9-inch square pan. Sprinkle with granulated sugar. Combine butter, flour, brown sugar, and oatmeal; sprinkle over berries. Bake at 350° for 30 minutes.

Passover Cheesecake

Crust:
1 1/2 cups crushed Matzo Meal
1 tablespoon cinnamon

Filling:
3 8-ounce packages cream
  cheese, softened

Glaze:
1 pint strawberries, divided
1/2 cup sugar

1/3 teaspoon salt
1/2 cup butter
1/3 cup sugar

4 eggs
1 cup sugar
1 teaspoon vanilla
1 tablespoon lemon juice

1 1/2 tablespoons potato starch
1 teaspoon lemon juice

(continued)

Passover Cheesecake   *(continued)*

Crust: Combine all ingredients and press into a 9-inch springform pan. Bake at 400° for 8 to 10 minutes.

Filling: Beat cream cheese; add eggs one at a time. Add sugar, vanilla and lemon juice. Beat for about 15 to 20 minutes, until very smooth. Pour into crust and bake at 375° for 40 minutes.

Glaze: Arrange 1 cup of whole or sliced strawberries on top of cake. Crush remaining berries; set aside. Combine sugar and potato starch in a saucepan; add crushed berries and lemon juice. Cook over medium heat until sauce is thick and clear. Press through a fine sieve and pour over cake.

Slovenian Noodle Strudel
Sheila Plevell, Aurora, Minnesota

1 8-ounce package noodles, 1/4-inch wide
3 eggs, beaten
1 cup sugar

2 pounds small curd creamy cottage cheese
2 cups golden raisins
1 cup sour cream

Topping:
1/2 cup graham cracker crumbs

2 tablespoons butter, melted

Cook and drain noodles; add eggs. Combine all remaining ingredients, add to noodle mixture and mix. Pour into a greased 9x13-inch baking dish. Smooth top with a spatula and sprinkle with topping.

Topping: Combine ingredients and mix well. Use to sprinkle over top of noodle mixture and bake at 350° for 1 hour.

Note: Can be used as a side dish with meat.

Rhubarb Whip

4 cups chopped rhubarb
1/2 cup sugar
1/4 cup water

1 3-ounce package strawberry gelatin
1/2 cup cold water
1/2 cup whipping cream, whipped
3 to 4 strawberries, halved

Combine rhubarb, sugar, and 1/4 cup water; bring to a boil. Cover and cook over medium heat for 10 minutes, stirring occasionally. Add gelatin and continue cooking and stirring until dissolved. Remove from heat and stir in cold water. Chill until partially set. Beat with an electric beater until fluffy. Fold in whipped cream. Pour into dessert dishes and chill until set. Garnish with strawberry halves. Serves 6 to 8.

Rhubarb Cake

1/2 cup butter or shortening
1 1/2 cups brown sugar
1/2 teaspoon salt
1 egg
1 teaspoon vanilla

2 cups flour
1 teaspoon baking soda
1 cup sour milk
1 1/2 cups chopped rhubarb
1/4 cup sugar
1 teaspoon cinnamon

Cream shortening and brown sugar. Add salt, egg, and vanilla. Sift together flour and baking soda. Add to first mixture alternately with sour milk. Fold in chopped rhubarb. Pour into a well-greased, 9x13-inch cake pan. Combine sugar and cinnamon; sprinkle cake with mixture. Bake at 375° for 30 to 35 minutes.

Rhubarb Cream Pie

Helga Mattson, Aurora, Minnesota

This is similar to the filling for a lemon meringue pie.

2 cups finely chopped rhubarb	2 eggs, separated
1 cup sugar, divided	2 tablespoons cornstarch
1/4 cup butter	1/4 cup light cream or milk
	1 9-inch baked pie shell

Combine rhubarb, 3/4 cup sugar, and butter; bring to a boil. Beat together egg yolks, cornstarch, and light cream. Stir about 1 cup of hot mixture into beaten yolk mixture. Add to remaining hot mixture and cook until thick and bubbly. Pour into a baked pie shell. Beat egg whites until foamy; add remaining sugar and beat until stiff peaks are formed. Spread over pie and bake at 350° for 10 to 15 minutes.

Czech Poppyseed Coffeecake

1 package dry yeast
1/4 cup lukewarm water
2 eggs
1/4 cup sugar
1/4 cup butter, softened

1 teaspoon salt
3/4 cup warm water
3 cups flour, divided
1/2 teaspoon mace or vanilla
4 to 5 cups poppyseed filling

Dissolve yeast in water and set aside. Beat eggs with sugar. Add softened butter, salt, milk, 1 cup flour, and mace or vanilla. Beat again. Add yeast mixture and mix well. Place dough on floured board and knead in remaining flour. Knead dough until smooth and not sticky, about 10 minutes. Roll into a rectangle sheet, 1/2-inch thick. Spread poppyseed filling on dough, roll up dough starting from the long end and put in a well greased Bundt pan. Let rise until almost double. Bake at 350° for 45 minutes.

Trail Bars

Excellent for backpacking and winter camping.

1 cup dark corn syrup
1 cup sugar
1 cup peanut butter
1/4 teaspoon salt
1/2 cup salted peanuts

4 cups high-protein, low-sugar flake cereal such as Special K Cereal
1 cup raisins
1 cup chocolate chips
1/2 cup shelled salted sunflower seeds

Boil syrup and sugar together until sugar dissolves; add peanut butter and salt; stir until smooth. Pour over nuts, cereal, raisins, chips, and sunflower seeds, stirring to coat. Press into a greased 9x13-inch pan; cool. Cut into 20 bars.

Sunflower Seed Cookies

1 cup butter
3/4 cup granulated sugar
3/4 cup brown sugar
2 eggs
1 teaspoon vanilla

1 tablespoon brandy
1 teaspoon baking soda
1 1/2 cups flour
3 cups oatmeal
1 cup toasted sunflower seeds

Cream butter and sugars; add eggs, vanilla, and brandy. Combine baking soda, flour, oatmeal, and sunflower seeds. Add to first mixture and mix well. Drop by teaspoonfuls onto greased baking sheets. Bake at 350° for 10 to 12 minutes.

Oat Health Bars

1/2 cup butter
1 cup brown sugar
1 teaspoon vanilla

2 cups rolled oats
1/4 teaspoon salt
1 teaspoon baking powder

Melt butter and sugar in a medium-sized saucepan. Add vanilla; stir in oats, salt, and baking powder, mix well. Pour into well-greased, 8-inch square pan. Bake at 325° for 30 minutes. Cool and cut into squares.

Variations: Any combination of sunflower seeds, coconut, or nuts, up to 1 cup, may be added. Maple or almond flavoring may be substituted for vanilla.

Norwegian Rosettes

3 eggs
1/3 cup sugar
1 cup flour

1/2 cup milk
1/4 teaspoon salt
oil for frying
powdered sugar for sprinkling

Beat eggs and sugar together. Add flour, milk, and salt. Beat until smooth. Heat rosette iron in hot oil until hot. Dip iron in batter, making sure that the batter does not get over the top of the iron. Place iron into hot oil and cook rosette for about 1 minute; shake iron to remove the rosette. When rosette drops off, remove it from oil and place on absorbent paper to drain. Sprinkle with powdered sugar.

A State of Events and Places to Visit

The pages that follow offer a sampling of the events and sites in Minnesota. There are many more ethnic and food festivals. For more information contact Minnesota Office of Tourism, 100 Metro Square, 121 Seventh Place E., St. Paul, Minnesota 55101. Or telephone 1-800-675-3700, or 296-5029 in Twin Cities.

Albert Lea—Big Island Rendezvous: Re-creation of an annual gathering of French Canadian voyageurs and Native Americans to trade furs and other goods, to celebrate, and to compete in games. Bluegrass music, Native American music, dancing, black powder shoot, tepee village, traders' row, workshops, ethnic foods. At Helmer Myre State Park, September/October.

Alexandria—Kensington Runestone Museum.

Annandale—Minnesota Pioneer Park: A pioneer village, 1886 church, log houses, pioneer women exhibit, artifacts, and nature trails.

Apple Valley—Minnesota Zoo: 250 wild animals and 2,000 plant varieties.
Bemidji—Lake Bemidji State Park: A boardwalk through a bog; rare flowers; a swimming beach; 16 miles of hiking trails; wildlife.
- Bunyan House and Fireplace of States: Paul Bunyan artifacts; a fireplace built of stones from every state and Canadian province.

Bingham Lake—Jeffers Petroglyphs: Drawings by Native Americans from 3,000 B.C. to the 18th century.

Brainerd—Paul Bunyan Amusement Center: Rides and attractions.
- Lumbertown, U.S.A.: Replica of an 1870 village.

Brooklyn Park—Historical Farm: Turn-of-the-century restored farmstead.

Burnsville—Scandinavian Heritage Home: Scandinavian traditions.

Chanhassen—Chanhassen Dinner Theatre: Largest dinner theater complex in the nation.
- Minnesota Landscape Arboretum: 905 acres of hills, lakes, fields, formal gardens, marshland and trails. Fall Festival with tram tours.

Chisholm—Ironworld USA: Dance to ethnic music, relive the mining history. See Old World ethnic craft demonstrations and eat ethnic foods. See name performers in amphitheatre. Ride the Ironworld Railroad.
- Minnesota Museum of Mining.

Cokato—Cokato Museum: Scandinavian history collection of Carl Good folkart carvings; reconstructed log cabin.

Coon Rapids—Bunker Hills Wave Pool and water amusement park.

Duluth—Port City of Lake Superior.
- Zoological Gardens
- St. Louis County Heritage and Arts Center: In 1892 Duluth Union Depot.

Eden Prairie—Air Museum Planes of Fame: Restored WW II aircraft.

Elk River—Victorian Wedding Dance: A theatrical Victorian wedding followed by a pig roast and wedding dance. Held in September.
- Olive Kelley Farm: Restored farm on the Mississippi; farming techniques from 1850–1870. Many special events.

Ely—Molter Memorial Museum: named for Dorothy Molter, last resident of the Boundary Waters Canoe Area Wilderness.

Eveleth—United States Hockey Hall of Fame.

Fairfax—Fort Ridgely: Built to protect settlers from the Dakota Sioux.

Falcon Heights—Gibbs Farm Museum; Development of urban fringe farming.

Grand Marais—Grand Portage: Re-creation of 200-year-old fur-trading post.

Grand Rapids—Forest History Center: 1900 logging camp; special events.

- Itasca County Historical Museum: Exhibits—one of actress Judy Garland, who was born in Grand Rapids.

Granite Falls—Upper Sioux Agency: Helped Dakota Sioux in 1854; now an interpretation center.

Harmony—Niagara Cave: Features a 60-foot waterfall.

Hibbing—Paulucci Space Theater.
- Hibbing High Auditorium: A copy of New York City's Old Capitol Theater.
- Hull Rust Mahoning Mine—An open pit iron ore mine.

Hinckley—Outdoor entertainment includes hiking, biking, roller blading, canoeing, kayaking, snowmobiling, cross-country skiing, and snoe shoeing.

International Falls—Voyageurs National Park Headquarters.
- Grand Mound Interpretive Center, west of International Falls and Pelland: Massive burial mound of the prehistoric Laurel tribes; trails, museum.

Lake Itasca—Itasca State Park: Headwaters of the Mississippi River.

Le Sueur—Historical Sawmill: The only surviving sawmill in the state.
- Mayo House—Historic home of the founder of Mayo Clinic.

Lewiston—Arches Branch Museum: Rural history, buildings, crafts.

Little Falls—Boyhood home of Charles A. Lindbergh, first to fly solo across the Atlantic ocean.

(continued)

Madison—Lac Qui Parle County Fair, September.

Mankota—Land of Memories Park, September: The Mah-Kato Traditional PowWow has dancing and music.

- American Music Festival, November: Celebrates American music through film, concerts and panel presentations.
- Festival of Lights, the "Great Holiday Turn-On," November/December: "Taste of Mankato" festivals, singing, dancing, holiday foods.
- 1800s Historic Festival, November: Fur-traders, music, story-telling, demonstrations, crafts, artifacts.

Minneapolis—Godfrey House: Built in 1849, oldest residence in city.

- Aquatennial, 10 days in July: A grand celebration of Minnesota with sports competitions, parades on water, food tents, celebrities performing from a barge on the Mississippi River, fireworks, and more! The first Aquatennial was held in 1939.

(continued)

Minneapolis *(continued)*

- AIM Anniversary PowWow, Fort Snelling State Park, September: American Indian ceremonial dancing in traditional native dress; traditional crafts and foods; cultural activities.
- Bell Museum of Natural History—On Minneapolis campus, University of Minnesota.
- Eloise Butler Wildflower Garden.
- Minneapolis Institute of Arts.
- Minneapolis Planetarium.
- Minnehaha Depot—Restored 1890s railroad depot.
- Nicollet Mall—Tree-lined lane with fountains, flowers, and lamplight.
- Walker Art Center—An acclaimed collection of contemporary art.
- The Tyrone Guthrie Theater.
- American Swedish Institute—Largest Swedish ethnic museum in U.S., housed in a turn-of-the-century mansion.

Minneapolis *(continued)*
- Firefighter's Memorial Museum—Historic firefighting equipment, engines.
- John H. Stevens House—First permanent settler's home in Minneapolis.

Monticello—Little Mountain Settlement Museum: Ethnic folk settlement (1855-1870s), Norwegian, German, Swedish, and New England cabins. Chippewa County Historical Museum—a 22-building pioneer village.

Moorhead—Heritage Hjemkomst Interpretive Center: Viking ship replica that sailed Duluth to Norway 1982. Special events, Holiday Heritage Festival.

Mora—A taste of Sweden, with largest carved horses in Swedish Dalarna style.

Morton—Lower Sioux Agency: Tells the story of the Dakota Sioux.

Mountain Lake—Heritage Village: Mennonite settlers' village with 17 buildings and the Minneapolis Telephone Hall of Fame. Many special events.

New Ulm—Enormous statue of Arminius (Hermann), who vanquished three Roman legions in A.D. 9, a precursor of German nationhood.

New York Mills—Finn Creek Museum: Restored 1890 Finnish farmstead.
Nisswa—Deer Forest-Fantasyland: Amusement park with petting zoo.
Northfield—Rice County Threshing Show, September: Grain threshing and lumber sawing. Antique machinery.
- Defeat of Jesse James Days, September: Reenactment of foiled Jesse James bank raid in 1876. Arts, crafts, rodeo, tractor pull, parade, drum/bugle fest.

Oakdale—Auntie Clare's Doll Hospital: A doll hospital, museum, and shop.
Old Frontenac—American Museum of Wildlife Art: Examples of the best.
Osage—Village of the Smoky Hills: Old-fashioned village, crafts from the past.
Park Rapids—Sawmill Creek: 1890s lumber town; operation farm; events.
Pine City—North West Company Fur Post: 1804-1805 wintering fur post.
Pipestone—Pipestone National Monument: Pipestone quarry has been used by Native Americans for centuries. Pipestone, a soft red rock, is used in making pipes and ornaments. *(continued)*

Pipestone *(continued)*
- Pipestone County Historical Museum: Indian artifacts; tour of downtown.

Red Wing—The Pottery Building: Famous Red Wing pottery was made here.

Rochester—Mayo Clinic: World-renowned medical center.
- Mayowood—55-room mansion; 3,000 acres. Home to 2 Mayo generations.
- Silver Lake, north of downtown—Home of thousands of Canadian geese.

Sauk Centre—Boyhood home of author Sinclair Lewis; museum.

Scandia—Gammelgarden Museum: State's oldest (1856) Lutheran Church building; first parsonage; farm buildings; shop with crafts, Swedish imports.

Shakopee—Minnesota Renaissance Festival, weekends August-September: re-creation of sixteenth-century harvest fest; costumes, musicians, jousting, artisans, foods, games.
- Valleyfair Family Amusement park: 60-acres of rides and attractions.
- Canterbury Downs—Pari-mutuel thoroughbred horse-racing track.

(continued)

Shakopee   *(continued)*
- Murphy's Landing—Living history museum with costumed guides; a pioneer village; farms; Dakota Sioux village.

Spring Valley—Mystery Cave: Twelve miles of connected caverns; tours.

St. Louis Park—Pavek Museum of Wonderful Wireless: Hundreds of vintage radios; displays of military communications equipment, horn-and-cone-type speakers; amateur radio station open to visiting amateur operators.

St. Paul—Minnesota State Fair: One of nation's largest. August/September.
- Great River Ride—Three-day, 150-mile September bike trek along Mississippi River from St. Paul to Winona.
- Science Museum of Minnesota and Omni Theater.
- Burbank-Livingston-Griggs House: Lavish Victorian version of Italian villa.
- Como Zoo.
- Como Park Conservatory.
- The Children's Museum.

St. Paul *(continued)*
- Minnesota Museum of Art.
- Minnesota Historical Society.
- Cathedral of St. Paul—Baroque-style cathedral built 1906-1915.
- James J. Hill House—Restored mansion (1891) of a railroad mogul.
- Fort Snelling/Fort Snelling History Center: Restored 1820s fort; costumed guides; role-playing civilians, soldiers. Military drill, tours. Special events.
- Old Muskego Church—First (1844) church built by Norwegians in America.
- Alexander Ramsey House—Victorian home of governor, senator and secretary of war Ramsey.
- Sibley and Faribault Houses—Minnesota's first governor lived in Sibley House; Faribault House belonged to a fur trader.
- Twin City Model Railroad Club: Railroads of the 1930s, 1940s and 1950s.

(continued)

St. Paul *(continued)*
- Stroh Brewing Company—Family owned and operated brewery.
- Minnesota State Capitol.
- Festival of Nations, in May: State's largest ethnic celebration; 43 authentic cafés; folk dancing; exhibits; folk art demonstrations; international bazaar.
- Taste of Minnesota—Food, music, and fireworks in June/July.
- Winter Carnival, January/February—Celebrating winter with parades, ice-carving, snow sculpting, contests, a puppet theater, royalty, and more.

Stillwater—Warden's House Museum, near the remains of the first territorial prison, is run by the Washington County Historical Society.

Taylors Falls—Dalles: Potholes created in prehistoric times.
- Folsom House—Original Folsom family furnishings in Greek-revival house.

Thief River Falls—Pennington County Pioneer Village: Log cabins, museum, railroad depots, schoolhouse, church, post office, store, and blacksmith shop.

Two Harbors—Split Rock Lighthouse on Lake Superior: Built in 1910, now a state park.

Vineland—Mille Lacs Indian Museum: Describes life of the region's Native Americans.

Walnut Grove—Laura Ingalls Wilder Museum: Dedicated to author of "Little House on the Prairie," who lived on Plum Creek in Walnut Grove.

White Bear Lake—Fillebrown House: Chalet-style 1879 house; antique furniture; Victorian clothing; memorabilia.

Winona—Victorian Fair: 19th-century crafts, food and music at historic homes and other sites.

- Polish Museum: "An echo of the past and a promise for the future." Events.

Worthington—State Corn Husking Contest, September. Champion huskers compete at the Nobels County Fairgrounds.

St. Urho's Day

Finnish-Americans cherish the folkways brought by their forefathers, but one bit of folklore that was lacking was a patron saint, such as the one celebrated by the Irish on St. Patrick's Day. So Finnish-Americans in Minnesota invented St. Urho's Day.

Now the governors of 50 states have proclaimed March 16 as St. Urho's Day. Each year, more happy celebrants turn out for the events. Costumes of nile green and royal purple have made those the colors of the day.

Thanks are offered to the legendary St. Urho for saving the grape crop of Finland from grasshoppers by shouting: "*Heinäsirkka, heinäsirkka, mene täältä hiiteen*" (grasshopper, grasshopper, go away from here). Sure enough, there are no grasshoppers in Finland.

St. Urho's Day offers Americans of Finnish descent an opportunity for fun and celebration, especially in cold snow country where the Ides of March can be quite drab.

Paul Bunyan

No state can match Minnesota for lasting enthusiasm in adopting the legends of Paul Bunyan, the mythical hero of the lumber camps. He was the tallest, the largest, the strongest of all. His fame is perpetuated by stories and statues. Of the latter, one of the largest is at Bemidji. In the lumber camps, the Paul Bunyan stories were larger than life but never larger than Bunyan. So much was written about him that scholars wondered if he was really a creature of oral folklore. But he was famous long before the writers discovered him, starting early in this century. Bunyan stories have been written by Esther Shephard, W. B. Laughead, and James MacGillivray. Carl Sandburg and Robert Frost wrote poems, and so did Richard Wilbur. W. H. Auden and Benjamin Britten produced an operetta. The theme never varies. Paul Bunyan lives on as the mythical hero of the lumber camps. He was the "mostest" of all.

Notes

Notes

Notes

BOOKS BY MAIL Penfield Stocking Stuffers: You may mix titles. Postpaid: One book for $12; 2 for $20; 3 for $28; 4 for $35; 6 for $50; 12 for $90. Complete catalog of all titles $2.50. *(Prices and availability subject to change.)* Please call 1-800-728-9998.

- Æbleskiver and More (Danish)
- Dandy Dutch Recipes
- Dutch Style Recipes
- Dear Danish Recipes
- Fine Finnish Foods
- German Style Recipes
- Great German Recipes
- Norwegian Recipes
- Scandinavian Holiday Recipes
- Scandinavian Smorgasbord Recipes
- Scandinavian Style Fish and Seafood Recipes
- Scandinavian Sweet Treats
- Splendid Swedish Recipes
- Time-Honored Norwegian Recipes
- Waffles, Flapjacks, Pancakes
- Slavic Specialties
- Pleasing Polish Recipes
- Cherished Czech Recipes
- Czech & Slovak Kolaches & Sweet Treats
- Quality Czech Mushroom Recipes
- Quality Dumpling Recipes
- Amish Mennonite Recipes & Traditions
- American Gothic Cookbook
- Recipes from Ireland
- Recipes from Old Mexico
- Savory Scottish Recipes
- Ukrainian Recipes
- Tales from Texas Tables
- Texas Cookoff

License to Cook Series:
Italian Style; Texas Style;
Alaska Style; Arizona Style;
Iowa Style; Minnesota Style;
New Mexico Style; Oregon Style;
Wisconsin Style

PENFIELD BOOKS • 215 BROWN STREET • IOWA CITY, IA 52245-5801 • WWW.PENFIELDBOOKS.COM